REPORTING QUALITATIVE RESEARCH IN PSYCHOLOGY

APA Style Products

Publication Manual of the American Psychological Association, Sixth Edition

Concise Rules of APA Style, Sixth Edition

Reporting Quantitative Research in Psychology: How to Meet APA Style Journal Article Reporting Standards, Second Edition
    Harris Cooper

Reporting Qualitative Research in Psychology: How to Meet APA Style Journal Article Reporting Standards
    Heidi M. Levitt

Presenting Your Findings: A Practical Guide for Creating Tables, Sixth Edition
    Adelheid A. M. Nicol and Penny M. Pexman

Displaying Your Findings: A Practical Guide for Creating Figures, Posters, and Presentations, Sixth Edition
    Adelheid A. M. Nicol and Penny M. Pexman

Mastering APA Style: Instructor's Resource Guide, Sixth Edition

Mastering APA Style: Student's Workbook and Training Guide, Sixth Edition

APA Style Guide to Electronic References, Sixth Edition

Please visit **http://www.apastyle.org/products/index.aspx** for more information about APA Style products or to order.

REPORTING QUALITATIVE RESEARCH IN PSYCHOLOGY

How to Meet
APA Style Journal
Article Reporting
Standards

HEIDI M. LEVITT

AMERICAN PSYCHOLOGICAL ASSOCIATION
Washington, DC

The opinions and statements published are the responsibility of the authors, and such opinions and statements do not necessarily represent the policies of the American Psychological Association.

Published by
American Psychological Association
750 First Street, NE
Washington, DC 20002
www.apa.org

APA Order Department
P.O. Box 92984
Washington, DC 20090-2984
Phone: (800) 374-2721; Direct: (202) 336-5510
Fax: (202) 336-5502; TDD/TTY: (202) 336-6123
Online: http://www.apa.org/pubs/books
E-mail: order@apa.org

In the U.K., Europe, Africa, and the Middle East, copies may be ordered from
Eurospan Group
c/o Turpin Distribution
Pegasus Drive
Stratton Business Park
Biggleswade, Bedfordshire
SG18 8TQ United Kingdom
Phone: +44 (0) 1767 604972
Fax: +44 (0) 1767 601640
Online: https://www.eurospanbookstore.com/apa
E-mail: eurospan@turpin-distribution.com

Typeset in Sabon, Futura, and Universe by Circle Graphics, Inc., Reisterstown, MD

Printer: Sheridan Books, Chelsea, MI
Cover Designer: Naylor Design, Washington, DC

Library of Congress Cataloging-in-Publication Data

Names: Levitt, Heidi M., author.
Title: Reporting qualitative research in psychology : how to meet apa style
  journal article reporting standards / by Heidi M. Levitt.
Description: First Edition. | Washington, DC : American Psychological
  Association, [2019] | Includes bibliographical references and index.
Identifiers: LCCN 2018033956 (print) | LCCN 2018036488 (ebook) | ISBN
  9781433830044 (eBook) | ISBN 1433830043 (eBook) | ISBN 9781433830037
  (pbk.) | ISBN 1433830035 (pbk.)
Subjects: LCSH: Psychology—Research—Methodology. | Qualitative
  research—Methodology.
Classification: LCC BF76.5 (ebook) | LCC BF76.5 .L458 2019 (print) | DDC
  150.72—dc23
LC record available at https://lccn.loc.gov/2018033956

British Library Cataloguing-in-Publication Data
A CIP record is available from the British Library.

Printed in the United States of America

http://dx.doi.org/10.1037/0000121-000
10 9 8 7 6 5 4 3 2 1

Contents

Acknowledgments

I would like to thank the members of the American Psychological Association Publications and Communications Board Working Group on Journal Article Reporting Standards for Qualitative Research as our work together provided the foundation for this book. Members include Michael Bamberg, John W. Creswell, David M. Frost, Ruthellen Josselson, and Carola Suárez-Orozco. Also, I would like to thank the coauthors of the Society for Qualitative Inquiry in Psychology's white paper on recommendations for the design and review of qualitative research, whose work contributed toward these standards: Sue L. Motulsky, Frederick J. Wertz, Susan L. Morrow, and Joseph G. Ponterotto. In addition, I would like to thank Scott Churchill, Michelle Fine, Ruthellen Josselson, Linda McMullen, and Frederick Wertz for their helpful comments and suggestions on segments of this book. I also thank Rose Sokol-Chang, Linda Malnasi McCarter, and David Becker for their support of these projects and the authors whose articles provide the examples that appear throughout the text. On a personal note, I thank Gloria, Tamara, and Shoshanna Levitt and Sharon Horne, Eden Levitt-Horne, and Joshua Levitt-Horne.

REPORTING
QUALITATIVE
RESEARCH IN
PSYCHOLOGY

Reporting Standards for Qualitative Research in Psychology: What Are They, and Why Do We Need Them?

Everyone loves a good story. A well-written or well-told story can draw you in and make you care about an issue that you never considered before. It can open new doors and change relationships by helping you understand others' experiences more deeply. It can teach you to develop empathy or imagine how you might feel if you were in a certain situation, time, or place. It can affirm reactions you have had and values to which you aspire, and it can provide guidance on the type of person you would like to be.

Before I learned about qualitative research, I would turn to novels and short stories when I faced complex dilemmas in my life. There, I could see how people suffered through heartbreak, found inspiration, and overcame hardships. When trying to understand myself, significant others, or clients, I did the same. Experiences that were not making sense would become clearer as I could see how parts of a story fit within a holistic account of how a person or a group of people made sense of themselves over time.

Strong qualitative research can have these same effects on its readers, deepening their understanding of complex processes and guiding them to respond to an issue in a new manner. The qualitative reporting standards described in this book were designed to guide authors and reviewers to think through how to strengthen the presentation of their work to increase its impact. I encourage you, as you read this book, to consider how these standards can help you communicate the story of your research more clearly and persuasively.

http://dx.doi.org/10.1037/0000121-001
Reporting Qualitative Research in Psychology: How to Meet APA Style Journal Article Reporting Standards, by H. M. Levitt

What Are Qualitative Journal Article Reporting Standards?

Qualitative researchers are interested not only in telling stories but also in developing knowledge to answer questions or solve problems. Once they have concluded their research and gained new understandings, they want to communicate this information to their field so that it can be used by others. *Reporting standards* are guidelines that describe how to communicate findings clearly in journal articles so that readers can access and understand the story of the research endeavor.

Recognizing that reporting standards can aid authors in the process of writing and evaluating manuscripts and editors and reviewers in the process of evaluating those manuscripts, the Publications and Communications (P&C) Board of the American Psychological Association (APA) invited two task forces of researchers to develop standards for reporting quantitative and qualitative research in journal articles. The Quantitative Journal Article Reporting Standards (JARS–Quant) Working Group (Mark Appelbaum [chair], Harris Cooper, Rex B. Kline, Evan Mayo-Wilson, Arthur M. Nezu, and Stephen M. Rao) developed standards for quantitative research (Appelbaum et al., 2018), and a separate book (Cooper, 2018) details those standards.

The development of reporting standards for qualitative methods was an initiative that was important to the P&C Board because use of these methods has increased rapidly in the field of psychology. There are so many qualitative methods in use, framed within multiple philosophical frameworks, that it can be challenging for journal reviewers who are unfamiliar with qualitative methods to evaluate whether a manuscript should be published. Reviewers who are unfamiliar with qualitative methods entirely or familiar with only one method or one tradition of inquiry may inappropriately use that knowledge to evaluate research that uses a different method or tradition. Others may adhere to incongruous criteria that are based within quantitative standards. Similarly, editors who do not have a background in qualitative research may be at a loss on how to adjudicate when reviews of a manuscript differ. This state of affairs has meant that it can be quite challenging to publish high-quality qualitative research.

To develop these standards, the P&C Board convened six researchers (Heidi M. Levitt [chair], Michael Bamberg, John W. Creswell, David Frost, Ruthellen Josselson, and Carola Suárez-Orozco) who had experience in using a variety of qualitative methods on a diverse range of topics and shared experience in journal editing. The Working Group on Journal Article Reporting Standards for Qualitative Research (JARS–Qual) considered readings related to qualitative reporting (e.g., Levitt, Motulsky, Wertz, Morrow, & Ponterotto, 2017; Madill & Gough, 2008; O'Brien, Harris, Beckman, Reed, & Cook, 2014; Tong, Sainsbury, & Craig, 2007; Walsh, 2015), met in person to form the core of the standards, then worked together remotely to develop recommendations. They sought feedback on these recommendations from the P&C Board, the APA Council of Editors, and the International Committee of the Society for Qualitative Inquiry in Psychology. In addition, they presented initial standards at an APA convention to invite feedback from the general membership (Levitt, Bamberg, et al., 2016). The final standards were published in *American Psychologist* (Levitt, Bamberg, et al., 2018).

This book is based on the reporting standards developed by this group. An advantage of this book is that it permits the space to expand on the ideas in those standards and to articulate the rationale behind each. Knowing these rationales can be helpful as you write up your own qualitative research as they will assist you in making decisions about how to interpret the standards.

How to Use This Book to Improve Your Research

This book describes the distinctive elements of qualitative reporting and goes beyond what is presented in the *American Psychologist* article on qualitative reporting (Levitt, Bamberg, et al., 2018) and the *Publication Manual of the American Psychological Association* (6th ed.; APA, 2010). It articulates decisions you may need to make as an author as you decide how to present your work. It also provides examples to illustrate a strong presentation style, and these can serve as helpful models. It does not review all the information in the *Publication Manual* on writing style, so that book will be a helpful guide as well.

Chapters 2 and 3 provide the conceptual undergirding for the reporting decisions that authors make during the writing process. Chapter 2 describes how the reporting of qualitative research is influenced by the purpose of a research project and the research traditions in use. For instance, constructivist authors writing up a participatory action study might intertwine their Method and Discussion sections as a way to highlight the coconstruction of the findings and their implications and to avoid a style of presentation that suggests that the results are objective while the discussion is subjective. Their approach to inquiry and their research tradition might guide them to present their work in a manner that highlights the strengths of their work in relation to their goals and as they are conceived within their tradition.

In Chapter 3, the concept of methodological integrity is discussed. Understanding this concept is critical to successful writing on qualitative research. It guides authors to report idiosyncratic aspects of their research in a way that conveys their rigor and also to explain how they addressed gaps in integrity.

Chapters 4 through 7 consider the typical sections of a qualitative research paper—the introductory sections, Method, Results, and Discussion. These chapters emphasize aspects of reporting that are unique to qualitative research. They describe the general elements that should be reported in qualitative papers and can assist authors in developing comprehensive reports that will support their review. Guidance is provided for how to best present qualitative research, with rationales and illustrations.

The reporting standards for qualitative meta-analyses, which are integrative analyses of findings from across primary qualitative research, are presented in Chapter 8. These standards are distinct from the standards for both quantitative meta-analyses and primary qualitative research. The chapter helps authors understand what is necessary to include in these reports.

Mixed methods studies use both qualitative and quantitative methods. Chapter 9 describes the reporting standards for this form of research. Although the reporting standards for mixed methods research draw on the standards for both quantitative and qualitative research, they emphasize the need to report how these methods work together to enhance understanding.

Finally, Chapter 10 includes a discussion of objectivist and constructivist rhetorical styles in research reporting. It encourages researchers to consider how the phrasing of their writing communicates their approach to inquiry and to engage readers using a style that is coherent with their approach. Also, this chapter describes the process of communicating with journal editors during the process of submitting a manuscript for review, emphasizing issues that tend to arise when submitting qualitative research and providing tips to facilitate the review. Finally, it describes future directions for qualitative research reporting as receptivity to and understanding of qualitative methods continue to increase.

Three tables listing the JARS–Qual guidelines are presented in this book. Shortened forms of these tables can be found online (http://www.apastyle.org/jars/). I also include text boxes that excerpt portions of the JARS–Qual tables that are relevant to the topic of each subsection, as appropriate. Table A1.1, in the appendix to this chapter, presents the general qualitative standards. In the appendix to Chapter 8, the table presenting reporting standards for qualitative meta-analyses can be found. The appendix to Chapter 9 contains the table of reporting standards for mixed methods research, as well as a table that presents the JARS–Quant guidelines essential to understand when reporting a mixed methods study. As you read the text, these tables will be a helpful reference.

You will notice that the JARS–Qual tables have three columns, whereas the JARS–Quant table has only two. The first column of the JARS–Qual tables contains the element of the article to be reported. The divisions in this column suggest sections and subsections that can be used to structure an article (e.g., introduction, objectives, methods), but the tables also note that qualitative researchers sometimes alter or combine sections and may opt to use a narrative format in papers. The second column of the tables contains a description of the information to be reported. Whether sections follow the outline in the JARS–Qual guidelines or are combined, the information related to each element should be reported in the paper. The third column contains recommendations and tips that can be useful for authors and reviewers to consider.

Understanding the rationale behind the reporting standards can help you make sense of how to apply a standard within your own project. As will be described, some of the standards may be adapted to better fit certain modes of research. As a researcher, you know your research best, and there may be ways you can support the methodological integrity of your work that are unique to your study and are not listed in the standards (which are meant to apply across qualitative studies). Be attuned to the modes of presentation that may strengthen your work and allow the story you are telling to be received as meaningful, innovative, and credible.

In addition, by describing the rationale for the standards, this book can help you explain your reporting decisions to reviewers or editors. There are many places in the reporting standards where we indicate that flexibility should be honored. In this book, I describe why a given standard might not hold for all studies, and you may wish to draw on these explanations in not only the writing process but the review process as well. Understanding the rationale for variations in reporting can assist you in crafting responses to reviewers and help reviewers and editors better understand your decisions. Because this book explains the thinking behind the standards developed by experts in qualitative methods in psychology, basing your explanations on this thinking can help you be persuasive when submitting your papers to peer review or responding to editors.

Appendix 1.1:
Journal Article Reporting Standards for All Qualitative Research Designs (JARS–Qual)

Table A1.1. Journal Article Reporting Standards for Qualitative Research (JARS–Qual): Information Recommended for Inclusion in Manuscripts That Report Primary Qualitative Research

Paper section or element	Description of information to be reported	Recommendations for authors to consider and notes for reviewers
Title page		
Title	• Identify key issues/topic under consideration.	
Author note	• Acknowledge funding sources or contributors. • Acknowledge conflicts of interest, if any.	
Abstract	• State the problem/question/objectives under investigation. • Indicate the study design, including types of participants or data sources, and analytic strategy, main results/findings, and main implications/significance. • Identify five keywords.	• *Authors:* Consider including at least one keyword that describes the method and one that describes the types of participants or phenomenon under investigation. • *Authors:* Consider describing your approach to inquiry when it will facilitate the review process and intelligibility of your paper. If your work is not grounded in a specific approach to inquiry or your approach would be too complicated to explain in the allotted word count, however, it would not be advisable to provide explication on this point in the abstract.
Introduction		
Description of research problem or question	• Frame the problem or question and its context. • Review, critique, and synthesize the applicable literature to identify key issues/debates/theoretical frameworks in the relevant literature to clarify barriers, knowledge gaps, or practical needs.	• *Reviewers:* The introduction may include case examples, personal narratives, vignettes, or other illustrative material.

| Study objectives/aims/research goals | • State the purpose(s)/goal(s)/aim(s) of the study.
• State the target audience, if specific.
• Provide the rationale for fit of design used to investigate this purpose/goal (e.g., theory building, explanatory, developing understanding, social action, description, highlighting social practices).
• Describe the approach to inquiry, if it illuminates the objectives and research rationale (e.g., descriptive, interpretive, feminist, psychoanalytic, postpositivist, critical, postmodern, or constructivist, or pragmatic approaches). | • *Authors*: If relevant to objectives, explain the relation of the current analysis to prior articles/publications.
• *Reviewers*: Qualitative studies often legitimately need to be divided into multiple manuscripts because of journal article page limitations, but each manuscript should have a separate focus.
• *Reviewers*: Qualitative studies tend not to identify hypotheses, but research questions and goals. |
| **Method**
Research design overview | • Summarize the research design, including data collection strategies, data analytic strategies, and, if illuminating, approaches to inquiry (e.g., descriptive, interpretive, feminist, psychoanalytic, postpositivist, critical, postmodern, constructivist, or pragmatic approaches).
• Provide the rationale for the design selected. | • *Reviewers*: Method sections can be written in a chronological or narrative format.
• *Reviewers*: Although they provide a method description that other investigators should be able to follow, it is not required that other investigators arrive at the same conclusions, but rather that their method should lead them to conclusions with a similar degree of methodological integrity.
• *Reviewers*: At times, elements may be relevant to multiple sections and authors need to organize what belongs in each subsection in order to describe the method coherently and reduce redundancy. For instance, the overview and the objectives statement may be presented in one section.

(table continues) |

Table A1.1. (*Continued*)

Paper section or element	Description of information to be reported	Recommendations for authors to consider and notes for reviewers
		• *Reviewers:* Processes of qualitative research are often iterative versus linear, may evolve through the inquiry process and may move between data collection and analysis in multiple formats. As a result, data collection and analysis sections might be combined.
		• *Reviewers:* For the reasons above and because qualitative methods often are adapted and combined creatively, requiring detailed description and rationale, an average qualitative Method section typically is longer than an average quantitative Method section.
Study participants or data sources		
Researcher description	• Describe the researchers' backgrounds in approaching the study, emphasizing their prior understandings of the phenomena under study (e.g., interviewers, analysts, or research team).	• *Authors:* Prior understandings relevant to the analysis could include, but are not limited to, descriptions of researchers' demographic/cultural characteristics, credentials, experience with phenomena, training, values, and decisions in selecting archives or material to analyze.
	• Describe how prior understandings of the phenomena under study were managed and/or influenced the research (e.g., enhancing, limiting, or structuring data collection and analysis).	• *Reviewers:* Researchers differ in the extensiveness of reflexive self-description in reports. It may not be possible for authors to estimate the depth of description desired by reviewers without guidance.

Participants or other data sources	• Provide the numbers of participants/documents/events analyzed. • Describe the demographics/cultural information, perspectives of participants or characteristics of data sources that might influence the data collected. • Describe existing data sources, if relevant (e.g., news-papers, Internet, archive). • Provide data repository information for openly shared data, if applicable. • Describe archival searches or process of locating data for analyses, if applicable.	
Researcher–participant relationship	• Describe the relationships and interactions between researchers and participants relevant to the research process and any impact on the research process (e.g., was there a relationship prior to research, are there any ethical considerations relevant to prior relationships).	
Participant recruitment Recruitment process	• Describe the recruitment process description (e.g., face-to-face, telephone, mail, email, recruitment protocols). • Describe any incentives or compensation, and provide assurance of relevant ethical processes of data collection and consent process as relevant (may include institutional review board approval, particular adaptations for vulnerable populations, safety monitoring). • Describe the process via which the number of participants was determined in relation to the study design. • Provide any changes in numbers through attrition and final number of participants/sources (if relevant, refusal rates or reasons for dropout). • Describe the rationale for decision to halt data collection (e.g., saturation). • Convey the study purpose as portrayed to participants, if different from the purpose stated.	• *Reviewers:* There is no agreed-upon minimum number of participants for a qualitative study. Rather, the author should provide a rationale for the number of participants chosen. • *Authors/Reviewers:* The order of the recruitment process and the selection process and their contents may be determined in relation to the authors' methodological approach. Some authors will determine a selection process and then develop a recruitment method based on those criteria. Other authors will develop a recruitment process and then select participants responsively in relation to evolving findings.

(*table continues*)

Table A1.1. (*Continued*)

Paper section or element	Description of information to be reported	Recommendations for authors to consider and notes for reviewers
Participant selection	• Describe the participants/data sources selection process (e.g., purposive sampling methods such as maximum variation, diversity sampling, or convenience sampling methods such as snowball selection, theoretical sampling) and inclusion/exclusion criteria. • Provide the general context for the study (when data were collected, sites of data collection). • If your participant selection is from an archived data set, describe the recruitment and selection process from that data set as well as any decisions in selecting sets of participants from that data set.	• *Authors:* A statement can clarify how the number of participants fits with practices in the design at hand, recognizing that transferability of findings in qualitative research to other contexts is based in developing deep and contextualized understandings that can be applied by readers rather than quantitative estimates of error and generalizations to populations. • *Authors/Reviewers:* The order of the recruitment process and the selection process and their contents may be determined in relation to the authors' methodological approach. Some authors will determine a selection process and then develop a recruitment method based upon those criteria. Other authors will develop a recruitment process and then select participants responsively in relation to evolving findings.

Data collection

Data collection/identification procedures

- State the form of data collected (e.g., interviews, questionnaires, media, observation).
- Describe the origins or evolution of the data-collection protocol.
- Describe any alterations of data-collection strategy in response to the evolving findings or the study rationale.
- Describe the data-selection or data-collection process (e.g., were others present when data were collected, number of times data were collected, duration of collection, context).
- Convey the extensiveness of engagement (e.g., depth of engagement, time intensiveness of data collection).
- For interview and written studies, indicate the mean and range of the time duration in the data-collection process (e.g., interviews were held for 75 to 110 min, with an average interview time of 90 min).
- Describe the management or use of reflexivity in the data-collection process, as it illuminates the study.
- Describe questions asked in data collection: content of central questions, form of questions (e.g., open vs. closed).

- *Reviewers*: Researchers may use terms for data collection that are coherent within their research approach and process, such as *data identification, data collection, or data selection*. Descriptions should be provided, however, in accessible terms in relation to the readership.
- *Reviewers*: It may not be useful for researchers to reproduce all of the questions they asked in an interview, especially in the case of unstructured or semistructured interviews as questions are adapted to the content of each interview.

Recording and data transformation

- Identify data audio/visual recording methods, field notes, and transcription processes used.

Analysis

Data-analytic strategies

- Describe the methods and procedures used and for what purpose/goal.
- Explicate in detail the process of analysis, including some discussion of the procedures (e.g., coding, thematic analysis, etc.), with a principle of transparency.
- Describe coders or analysts and their training, if not already described in the researcher description section (e.g., coder selection, collaboration groups).

- *Reviewers*: Researchers may use terms for data analysis that are coherent within their research approach and process (e.g., *interpretation, unitization, eidetic analysis, coding*). Descriptions should be provided, however, in accessible terms in relation to the readership.

(table continues)

Table A1.1. (*Continued*)

Paper section or element	Description of information to be reported	Recommendations for authors to consider and notes for reviewers
	• Identify whether coding categories emerged from the analyses or were developed a priori. • Identify units of analysis (e.g., entire transcript, unit, text) and how units were formed, if applicable. • Describe the process of arriving at an analytic scheme, if applicable (e.g., if one was developed before or during the analysis or was emergent throughout). • Provide illustrations and descriptions of their development, if relevant. • Indicate software, if used.	• *Authors:* Provide rationales to illuminate analytic choices in relation to the study goals.
Methodological integrity	• Demonstrate that the claims made from the analysis are warranted and have produced findings with methodological integrity. The procedures that support methodological integrity (i.e., fidelity and utility) typically are described across the relevant sections of a paper, but they could be addressed in a separate section when elaboration or emphasis would be helpful. Issues of methodological integrity include the following: • Assess the *adequacy* of the data in terms of the ability to capture forms of diversity most relevant to the question, research goals, and inquiry approach.	• *Reviewers:* Research does not need to use all or any of the checks (as rigor is centrally based in the iterative process of qualitative analyses, which inherently includes checks within the evolving, self-correcting iterative analyses), but their use can augment a study's methodological integrity. Approaches to inquiry have different traditions in terms of using checks and which checks are most valued.

- Describe how the *researchers' perspectives* were managed in both the data collection and analysis (e.g., to limit their effect on the data collection, to structure the analysis).
- Demonstrate that findings are *grounded* in the evidence (e.g., using quotes, excerpts, or descriptions of researchers' engagement in data collection).
- Demonstrate that the contributions are *insightful* and *meaningful* (e.g., in relation to the current literature and the study goal).
- Provide relevant *contextual* information for findings (e.g., setting of study, information about participants, interview question asked is presented before excerpt as needed).
- Present findings in a *coherent* manner that makes sense of contradictions or disconfirming evidence in the data (e.g., reconcile discrepancies, describe why a conflict might exist in the findings).
- Demonstrate *consistency* with regard to the analytic processes (e.g., analysts may use demonstrations of analyses to support consistency, describe their development of a stable perspective, interrater reliability, consensus) or describe responses to inconsistencies, as relevant (e.g., coders switching midanalysis, an interruption in the analytic process). If alterations in methodological integrity were made for ethical reasons, explicate those reasons and the adjustments made.

(table continues)

Table A1.1. (*Continued*)

Paper section or element	Description of information to be reported	Recommendations for authors to consider and notes for reviewers

	• Describe how support for claims was supplemented by any checks added to the qualitative analysis. Examples of supplemental checks that can strengthen the research may include
	  • transcripts/data collected returned to participants for feedback;
	  • triangulation across multiple sources of information, findings, or investigators;
	  • checks on the interview thoroughness or interviewer demands;
	  • consensus or auditing process;
	  • member checks or participant feedback on findings;
	  • data displays/matrices;
	  • in-depth thick description, case examples, or illustrations;
	  • structured methods of researcher reflexivity (e.g., sending memos, field notes, diary, logbooks, journals, bracketing); and
	  • checks on the utility of findings in responding to the study problem (e.g., an evaluation of whether a solution worked).	

Findings/Results

Findings/Results subsections

- Describe research findings (e.g., themes, categories, narratives) and the meaning and understandings that the researcher has derived from the data analysis.
- Demonstrate the analytic process of reaching findings (e.g., quotes, excerpts of data).
- Present research findings in a way that is compatible with the study design.
- Present synthesizing illustrations (e.g., diagrams, tables, models), if useful in organizing and conveying findings. Photographs or links to videos can be used.

- *Reviewers:* Findings sections tend to be longer than in quantitative papers because of the demonstrative rhetoric needed to permit the evaluation of the analytic procedure.
- *Reviewers:* Depending on the approach to inquiry, findings and discussion may be combined or a personalized discursive style might be used to portray the researchers' involvement in the analysis.
- *Reviewers:* Findings may or may not include quantified information, depending upon the study's goals, approach to inquiry, and study characteristics.
- *Authors:* Findings presented in an artistic manner (e.g., a link to a dramatic presentation of findings) should also include information in the reporting standards to support the research presentation.
- *Reviewers:* Use quotes or excerpts to augment data description (e.g., thick, evocative description, field notes, text excerpts), but these should not replace the description of the findings of the analysis.

(table continues)

Table A1.1. (*Continued*)

Paper section or element	Description of information to be reported	Recommendations for authors to consider and notes for reviewers
Discussion		
Discussion subsections	• Describe the central contributions and their significance in advancing disciplinary understandings. • Describe the types of contributions made by findings (e.g., challenging, elaborating on, and supporting prior research or theory in the literature describing the relevance) and how findings can be best utilized. • Identify similarities and differences from prior theories and research findings. • Reflect on any alternative explanations of the findings. • Identify the study's strengths and limitations (e.g., consider how the quality, source, or types of the data or the analytic processes might support or weaken its methodological integrity). • Describe the limits of the scope of transferability (e.g., what readers should bear in mind when using findings across contexts). • Revisit any ethical dilemmas or challenges that were encountered, and provide related suggestions for future researchers. • Consider the implications for future research, policy, or practice.	• *Reviewers*: Accounts could lead to multiple solutions rather than a single one. Many qualitative approaches hold that there may be more than one valid and useful set of findings from a given data set.

Note. Adapted from "Journal Article Reporting Standards for Qualitative Primary, Qualitative Meta-Analytic, and Mixed Methods Research in Psychology: The APA Publications and Communications Board Task Force Report," by H. M. Levitt, M. Bamberg, J. W. Creswell, D. M. Frost, R. Josselson, and C. Suárez-Orozco, 2018, *American Psychologist, 73*, pp. 34–37. Copyright 2018 by the American Psychological Association.

2

Telling Your Qualitative Story: How the Purpose of Your Research Influences Your Reporting

Researchers engage in qualitative methods for varied purposes and construct projects to meet differing goals, processes that are relevant for qualitative research reporting. They convey their research stories for specific reasons that are meaningful to them and to their readers. Although I have long enjoyed designing quantitative research studies to test my ideas, it was when I discovered qualitative methods that I really began to consider being a researcher as a central occupational role. I was drawn to the ability to explore and communicate stories that were grounded in the complexity of people's lives. When beginning my academic career, it was incredible to me that through interviews, people who had expertise in issues that I found fascinating would share their experiences. I could learn from them and shape their knowledge and experience into an empirical narrative to be shared with others.

As my interests varied, so did my studies. At one point I was sitting in an ancient library located in the foothills of the Himalayas, drinking salt and butter tea and listening to monks describe wisdom while chanting prayers resounded through the monastery (Levitt, 1999). At another time, I was learning what it meant to be a femme lesbian and finding my own identity shifting and changing (Levitt, Gerrish, & Hiestand, 2003). In other studies, I discovered what clients find helpful during sessions but do not share with their therapists (Levitt, Butler, & Hill, 2006) and what master therapists consider as they tailor interventions to their clients' needs (e.g., Levitt & Williams, 2010). Holding central in my mind the goals of each study guided me as I engaged in writing the manuscripts. I reflected on my experience of engaging in the research, the logic of the methods I was using, and the tradition of inquiry within which I was working in an effort to increase the transparency of my process.

http://dx.doi.org/10.1037/0000121-002
Reporting Qualitative Research in Psychology: How to Meet APA Style Journal Article Reporting Standards, by H. M. Levitt

To communicate qualitative research coherently, it is not enough to detail the steps of a method; it is also important to understand the personal assumptions, methods, and traditions within which you are working and the way that they frame your inquiry. As I review the Journal Article Reporting Standards for Qualitative Research (JARS–Qual), you will see that guidance often is framed in relation to the researchers' goals, approach to inquiry, or methods. In this chapter, I review some of these central concepts so that it will make sense why they might influence research reporting and so that I can use these terms to facilitate the discussion of reporting throughout the book.

What Is Qualitative Research?

Qualitative research has been in use since the beginning of the field of psychology; however, it often went unpublished because it did not fit the accepted mode of scientific reporting of the time (Wertz, 2014). Profound shifts in psychological understanding have been advanced by qualitative research, such as Sigmund Freud's (1900) case studies, Abraham Maslow's (1968) studies on self-actualization, and Carol Gilligan's (1977) research on morality. These works generated tectonic shifts in the way the field conceptualized what it meant to be human (see Madill, 2015b; Wertz, 2014, for myriad examples of transformative early qualitative research).

As researchers have come to articulate systematic procedures for qualitative methods, the value of these methods has been increasingly recognized, and familiarity with them has grown (e.g., K. J. Gergen, Josselson, & Freeman, 2015). Over each of the past 5 decades, the number of articles and dissertations using these methods has rapidly increased (Ponterotto, 2005a, 2005c). Multiple journals for qualitative researchers have been established (e.g., *Qualitative Health Research, Qualitative Inquiry, Qualitative Psychology, Qualitative Research in Psychology*), and qualitative research is published in a wide range of mainstream journals as well. In 2011, Division 5: Quantitative and Qualitative Methods of the American Psychological Association (APA) established a subdivision focused on qualitative methods, the Society for Qualitative Inquiry in Psychology. In short, qualitative research methods have flourished in psychology, as they have in many social sciences. As this has occurred, the ways to report qualitative research have evolved and general expectations have developed.

Although the term *qualitative research* has come to encompass multiple methods and inquiry traditions, it brings together a set of methods that share four central characteristics:

1. Qualitative research involves the analysis of natural language and other forms of human expression (e.g., text, artistic products) rather than numbers. This form of data sets qualitative methods apart from statistical and mathematical analyses. This verbal description means that the data can capture processes or experiences that are ambiguous, inchoate, and complexly interrelated. Also, analyses of these data often go beyond any beliefs or assumptions researchers might have held prior to data collection to produce new insights, theories, descriptions, and understandings.

2. Qualitative methods centralize an iterative process—that is, data are analyzed and meanings are generated in a circular and repeating manner. As data are examined, an initial understanding of the meaning they contain is developed, and then

the meaning can be reexamined in the light of new data and refined. The understanding of the new data might shift the understanding of the already examined data or vice versa. Through this process, researchers gradually develop findings that can relay central aspects of the data they are examining.

3. Qualitative researchers seek to present their findings in a manner that emphasizes their context and situation in time. For instance, researchers strive to make explicit the time, place, culture, and interpersonal dynamics upon which their findings depend rather than to seek laws. In keeping with this ethic, they tend to present overtly the ways in which the processes they study are in flux, relational, or evolving in time so that consumers of the research can apply the findings adequately to their own situations.

4. Because qualitative methods are based on researchers' interpretation or description of patterns they perceive in the data, questions can be asked about the researchers' ability to engage in this task. In response, researchers using these approaches tend to report their findings with a rhetorical style that includes subjectivist disclosures (Levitt, Pomerville, Surace, & Grabowski, 2017). This means that researchers not only engage in self-reflection and consider how their perspectives and limitations might influence their research; they also describe these considerations and the steps they took to address any concerns, as described in the JARS–Qual guidelines. In these approaches, researchers' transparency about their positions and any relationships with participants contributes to readers' confidence in the research, as it demonstrates that the researchers either have taken care to limit the effects of their own perspective on the research or are up-front about their perspectives so readers can understand the findings as coming from a certain position. More on this point is forthcoming in Chapter 3.

When reporting qualitative studies, it helps to have a clear understanding of these distinctive aspects of qualitative research. A few examples of common reporting strategies that reveal misunderstandings of qualitative methods include referring to participants as a "sample" when you did not use sampling theory to estimate a population, describing your assumptions as "hypotheses," or using language that decontextualizes your findings or suggests that they are natural laws that persist across time and culture. Using language that conflates qualitative methods with quantitative methods can obscure what you are doing and will undermine your credibility. When presenting mixed methods research within a single report, researchers should use the language that is consistent with the aspect of the research being presented in a given section (e.g., either qualitative or quantitative). You can consult the recommendations for mixed methods reporting in Chapter 9 for further details.

What Are Traditions of Inquiry?

Sometimes researchers view their methods as being conducted within philosophical frameworks that articulate the researchers' goals, values, and conceptions of the research process. Being able to articulate a tradition of inquiry can be useful in making clear the aims of a research project, which can influence how the project is evaluated in meeting its goals. You may see these traditions described in the literature alternately as epistemological beliefs, worldviews, paradigms, strategies, or research traditions

(Creswell, 2013a; Levitt, Bamberg, et al., 2018; Morrow, 2005; Ponterotto, 2005b). For instance, researchers might indicate that their approaches to inquiry are descriptive, interpretive, feminist, psychoanalytic, postpositivist, constructivist, critical, postmodern, or constructivist. Often qualitative research is presented without specifying an inquiry tradition, even when it is implicit. Whereas some research is decisively based in one of these traditions, research also may be based on a combination of these values, or it may be question driven and conducted pragmatically (Morgan, 2007).

Although theorists may divide these philosophies into different groupings (e.g., Creswell, 2013a; Guba & Lincoln, 2005; Madill & Gough, 2008; Mertens, 2010; Parker, 2004; Ponterotto, 2005a) and delineations of these approaches are not always clear (Staller, 2013), the following paragraphs provide a brief summary of the core features of four traditions of inquiry that are in common use—postpositivist, constructivist–interpretive, critical–ideological, and pragmatic—to highlight the diversity in their goals and illustrate how the reporting of qualitative research using these methods would be adjusted. These traditions are reviewed in more detail elsewhere (e.g., Morgan, 2007; Morrow, 2005; Ponterotto, 2005a).

For *postpositivist* researchers, science functions through the use of an objective approach to analysis in which researchers attempt to minimize error and biases in their observations. Goals of this research include rejecting or confirming theories, providing explanations, and enabling predictions. For example, educational researchers might decide to investigate how well the educational goal of teaching students to contrast perspectives is met when discussing great literary works in the English curriculum. They might describe training multiple researchers to identify types of perspective-taking in essays on assigned books and obtain interrater reliability on their coding to demonstrate that they are operationalizing and identifying the phenomenon in an objective manner. They might develop a system to identify the three main forms of perspective training to help teachers support and evaluate students who are learning this skill. In doing so, they would identify the types of perspective-taking that exist in students in such a way as to permit their reliable identification across investigators. Their discursive style when reporting their research would emphasize the objectivity and reliability of the researchers and might use the third person to minimize the appearance of subjectivity. Other discursive strategies that have characterized postpositivist research include the use of a neutral tone and the avoidance of descriptions that situate the researchers in terms of personal identities and prior experiences that are relevant to the research under way. Chapter 5 describes how methods can be described in keeping with these and other traditions of inquiry.

Constructivist–interpretive researchers believe that researchers and participants codevelop findings together through the inquiry process. Their goal is to uncover meanings while making transparent the interpretive processes that occur throughout their careful process of analysis. This means that these researchers not only consider their influence on their analyses but also report this process of forming results as a central part of their findings. If these researchers were interested in the question of how perspective-taking is learned via literature, they would not be as interested in demonstrating the interrater reliability of their observations because they wouldn't view the understanding of perspective-taking as something that exists independently of themselves. Instead, they would be interested in considering the ways through which they come to distinguish types of perspective-taking and how their process of interpretation evolves across their study or across time. They would be likely to report how they brought to their interpretive work implicit literary theories that led them to understand perspective-taking in light of those theories. For instance, a researcher who approached students' essays with a background in psychodynamic theory might generate distinct insights from a researcher with a behavioral or humanistic perspective. Discussion within the research team may lead each of the researchers to shift his or her understandings of the essays and to recognize new forms of perspective-taking.

For *critical–ideological* researchers, research is used to promote liberation, transformation, and social change, and this purpose overtly guides their data analysis and reporting. Research goals include documenting, unmasking, and disrupting privilege, power, and oppression. Critical researchers might conduct the study on the development of perspective-taking in literary works by looking at how the perspectives taken in novels coincide with or challenge socially dominant perspectives. Or they might look at student essays to see whether students are able to shift between perspectives of characters in dominant and marginalized positions. Can they adopt the perspective of people occupying contrasting social positions? Their questions might examine how readers come to be critical of social myths and embrace an understanding of marginalized perspectives. These approaches use some distinctive methods that are discussed in the next section.

Finally, researchers using a *pragmatic* approach tend not to identify with sets of philosophical assumptions about the research process but rather to use methods to achieve various practical aims. In this research, the goal is to solve specified problems and to yield consequences that can be of benefit (Patton, 2015). For instance, researchers might begin the literary works study with a mission to identify the most beneficial books for developing complexity of thinking about racial minority issues. They might combine a variety of methods or procedures to answer this question without having an investment in any of the epistemic questions about how people come to form understandings (McLeod, 2011). For instance, they could conduct a qualitative theme analysis to form a scale that they could then use to rate the complexity of thinking in responses to essay questions. They could analyze the ratings in relation to the textbooks assigned or examine books across decades. Their reporting style is problem focused—meaning that instead of adopting any one tradition of inquiry consistently, these researchers vary their approach and style of writing to focus on the most pressing concerns within each problem.

These summaries of four traditions of inquiry clearly are not exhaustive. They can, however, help you appreciate some of the distinct goals and traditions used in qualitative research.

What Are Qualitative Methods?

Although qualitative methods share the characteristics outlined in the previous section, there are a wide array of specific qualitative methods in use in psychological science. Methods often stem from varied approaches to analysis that include case study (e.g., Fishman & Westerman, 2011; Yin, 2014), consensual qualitative (e.g., Hill, 2012), conversational (e.g., Madill, Widdicombe, & Barkham, 2001), critical (e.g., Fine, 2013; Steinberg & Cannella, 2012), discursive (e.g., Madill, 2015a; Pea, 1993; Potter & Wetherell, 1987), ethnographic (e.g., Suzuki, Ahluwalia, Mattis, & Quizon, 2005; Wolcott, 2008), grounded theory (e.g., Charmaz, 2014; Glaser & Strauss, 1967), narrative (e.g., Bamberg, 2012; Josselson, Lieblich, & McAdams, 2007), phenomeno-logical (e.g., Giorgi, 2009; Smith, 2004), performative (e.g., M. M. Gergen & Gergen, 2012), and thematic (e.g., Braun & Clarke, 2006; Finfgeld-Connett, 2014), among others. Methods also could be differentiated by the way they organize data (e.g., into narratives, themes, performative acts, or conversational turns, as suggested by their names) or by their purposes (e.g., to develop theory, to describe phenomena, or to raise consciousness). In addition, many of these methods can take multiple forms because researchers may shift their philosophical assumptions or their procedures as their studies evolve (K. J. Gergen, 2014).

Although it is not possible to provide an in-depth description of the many methods in this book, which focuses on reporting standards, many strong textbooks offer overviews of qualitative methods (e.g., Creswell, 2013a; Gelo, Pritz, & Rieken, 2015; McLeod, 2011; Wertz et al., 2011), and many more texts provide a thorough description of one method.

Reviewers and readers will examine your report to decide whether you have adhered to the values, goals, and procedures within the approaches you have selected. The JARS–Qual guidelines, however, do not specify the specific procedures that should be reported for every qualitative method (which would make them unwieldy). Instead, researchers are expected to familiarize themselves with the methods they are using and to report in a manner that represents their features. In this section, I describe only a few methods to highlight some of the diversity in their goals and procedures (Levitt, 2016) to suggest how they might influence reporting. As will be seen, methods have specific vocabularies, procedures, and perspectives on the analytic process, and researchers want their reports to reflect these particularities. Also, it will be helpful to have some understanding of the distinctions among these approaches because I refer back to these methods in later chapters of this book.

Phenomenological Approaches to Method

The phenomenological tradition has enjoyed a longer research history than other quali-tative methods in modern psychology, following its development by Husserl (1925/1977) and its use in Europe during the 20th century (Wertz, 2015). Husserl's aim was to pro-vide a scientific method for studying experience that would achieve success comparable to investigations of physical nature using natural science methods. In the 1960s, Giorgi (2009) delineated and developed procedures for psychological research based on and modifying Husserl's methods at Duquesne University (see also Churchill, 2018; Churchill & Wertz, 2015). This approach involves setting aside theories, hypotheses, and assumptions (called *bracketing*) and reflectively focusing on the meanings and struc-tures of experience (a procedure called *intentional analysis*). Using a procedure called *free imaginative variation*, the researcher modifies the factual details of examples under analysis in order to grasp essential meanings of experience at higher levels of generality. The basic steps in this method, which uses interview-based, written, and observational descriptions of concrete examples of the subject matter, are open reading, demarcating meaning units, reflecting on psychological meanings, and synthesizing reflections in general structural descriptions (Giorgi, 2009).

Other influential approaches to phenomenological methods include interpretive phenomenological analysis (e.g., Smith, Flowers, & Larkin, 2009), which was devel-oped independently of empirical phenomenology. This approach is distinguished by its encouragement of researchers to use their preconceptions deliberately within their analyses (rather than to set them aside) and to engage with participants in codeveloping interpretations of their process of making meaning. Both approaches have gained in popularity and are being used in the United States and internationally to study a broad range of topics and issues. The JARS–Qual guidelines encourage researchers to transparently present in their writing their approach to the management of their perspectives and the interpretive process (see Chapters 4, 5, and 10 for further discussion).

Grounded Theory Approaches to Method

Like phenomenology, multiple versions of grounded theory have been produced that are based in distinctive traditions of inquiry and procedures (e.g., Bryant & Charmaz, 2010; Rennie, 2012), and even the originators of the method (e.g., Glaser & Strauss, 1967) went on to develop separate sets of procedures from one another. Grounded theory method approaches share a number of distinguishing factors, however. They share the analytic process of constant comparison, in which each unit of data is compared with every other unit. As researchers identify commonalities between the units, they group data into categories. Labels are generated for each category that are based on the common meanings therein. The labeled categories are compared with one another in turn, and higher order categories are developed and labeled to reflect their shared meanings. This process continues until a data hierarchy is formed that has at its apex a core category, which is the central finding of the analysis.

Other defining features of grounded theory include data collection being guided by *theoretical sampling methods*—in which investigators seek out participants strategically so as to flesh out their understanding within their ongoing analysis—and stopping at the point of *saturation*, which is when additional data no longer seem to bring new understandings to the analysis. These latter procedures have gained broad acceptance in the field and are now routinely incorporated into other qualitative methods as well (see Chapter 5 for information to report on data collection).

Narrative Approaches to Method

The focus on narrative came into psychology as cognitive psychologists began to conceptualize the brain as processing and encoding information in narrative rather than digital format (Bruner, 1990; Ricoeur, 1984). Narrative researchers tend to be less interested in the facticity of events than in the ways people construct and organize understandings. These methods have been embraced in varied areas of psychology, and researchers have developed a wide range of coding systems and qualitative methods (e.g., Angus & McLeod, 2004).

The narrative approach has expanded to include methodological variations that study the content of narratives, their function, their structural features, their evolution over time, and the process of producing them (e.g., Labov, 2006; Polkinghorne, 1988). Often narrative is viewed as a rhetorical device through which people represent experiences to both themselves and others in a manner situated in time and positioned in terms of cultural and relational dynamics. The social location of individuals, the sequencing of events, and the intentions of the author or of characters in a narrative all may be considered. Entire life stories can be examined, or studies can focus on stories told within or about people's lives or stories related to specific topics or concerns (e.g., Josselson, Lieblich, & McAdams, 2007). Narratives can be studied in isolation by studying their effect on listeners and by studying their meaning within their historical and cultural context.

The wide variety of procedures used under the narrative heading can provide some flexibility in adopting analytic procedures. The evolution of themes could be examined in relation to the passage of time, shifts in society, or the introduction of new plots or characters, and researchers could track various narrative processes in use. The patterns identified could be related to other stories to help researchers identify key features and processes of narratives of empowerment, for example. The JARS–Qual can be used to help researchers using these diverse narrative approaches make decisions about how to present their methods thoroughly.

Critical Approaches to Method

Although critical research can be considered a tradition of inquiry, researchers also tend to use certain procedures when they conduct qualitative research. They begin their analyses with an interest in how interpersonal and sociopolitical structures and processes (e.g., gender, race, ethnicity, sexual orientation, immigration status) function to support the privilege of dominant classes in society. Researchers are interested in shedding light on otherwise invisible forces of oppression and injustice that have become status quo (e.g., Fine, 2013). They also critique the research process and the ways the discipline of psychology engages in acts that might perpetuate discriminatory practices and perspectives (e.g., Wendt & Gone, 2012). Instead of being tied to one methodological approach, critical approaches often take the form of interpretive lenses through which various methods can be conducted (e.g., Chang & Yoon, 2011). Also, researchers tend to deliberately include participants and researchers who are from the communities they are investigating to bring these perspectives to their research. They often use qualitative methods among quantitative methods and other processes (see Chapter 9 on the Mixed Methods Article Reporting Standards), however, because of their distinct goals that center on social justice, institutional change, and empowerment rather than purely the generation of new knowledge.

Researchers would be especially interested in reporting findings from varied perspectives that might include youth with multiple types of marginalization (e.g., racial, ethnic, sexual), teachers, principals, parents, and psychologists from varied social positions. For this reason, influential others in the system tend to be invited to join the research team. Researchers might report on findings using a lens based in critical theory to convey the problems of how to support authenticity in at-risk youth systemically, hear one another's perspectives, develop research projects together, and identify routes to improve their systems.

Discursive Approaches to Method

Discourse analysts use qualitative methods to closely examine the functions of discourse but without the goal of uncovering the internal experience underlying its production (Potter, Edwards, & Wetherell, 1993). Discourse analysis encompasses approaches with varied epistemological foundations and practices (e.g., Riley, Sims-Schouten, & Willig, 2007). It is related to conversational analysis, although conversational analyses focus on dialogue to observe interactional processes (Madill, 2015a), and discursive analyses can examine patterns of text from a single source. Qualitative approaches to discourse analysis in psychology tend to incorporate a lens through which researchers explore how cultural and ideological assumptions make discourse intelligible (Parker, 2015). They engage in a close analysis of the words and phrases used in communication and their rhetorical impact. For instance, critical discourse researchers often begin from feminist and multicultural frameworks and, rather than seeking to set these perspectives aside, use them to shed light on oppressive or deceptive social practices and to further social justice aims. Chapter 3 provides detailed guidance on how to present research in a manner that has integrity in light of your research aims.

Researchers might examine how a discourse evolves by tracking its emergence. They would report on these competing discourses by examining how they play out and transform. Also, they explore the influence and impact of these discourses. Researchers might examine, for instance, how sexist discourses function to normalize the silencing and objectification of female rape victims in their testimonies. These approaches differ from linguistic quantitative approaches to discourse analysis that may use statistics to assess discursive features.

Summary: The Role of JARS–Qual

From these brief descriptions, it should be clear how qualitative method traditions may function distinctly and toward separate ends. Even from a cursory examination of just these few qualitative methods, it is striking that they have distinctive terminology, procedures, and goals. For instance, empirical phenomenologists would report on processes of epoché and reduction, grounded theorists would describe the process of developing a hierarchy and establishing saturation, narrative researchers would describe the ways they used narrative structures and processes to engage in their research, critical researchers would describe the theories they drew on as analytic tools, and discourse analysts would demonstrate evidence for the functions of discourses in conversations.

The JARS–Qual guidelines do not provide guidance at the level of each of these methodological approaches, meaning it is incumbent on researchers to learn the distinctive features of any method being used or to present a rationale for methods they develop. The language that researchers use throughout their reporting would reflect both their methods and their approach to inquiry. The role of JARS–Qual is to support researchers to make deliberate decisions about what information to include in their reporting across methods. These ideas continue to be discussed in the next chapter on methodological integrity.

3

Methodological Integrity: Establishing the Fidelity and Utility of Your Research

Researchers have long been concerned with communicating the rigor of their methods. Because there are many qualitative methods that might be embedded in diverse inquiry traditions, there can be multiple ideas on what makes a qualitative project any good. This issue is close to the hearts of qualitative researchers who wish to develop studies that are rigorous and generate confidence in their findings. Also, this issue is central when considering reporting standards for research because researchers need to know what should be reported to help readers understand both the strengths and the limitations of their study in relation to the ideal of rigor. But given all the diversity in approaches, how can rigor be assessed?

Methodological integrity is one of the most effective standards for measuring rigor, and it consists of two components that are considered in this chapter: *fidelity to the subject matter* and *utility of research contributions*. The Journal Article Reporting Standards for Qualitative Research (JARS–Qual) discuss methodological integrity within the context of the Method section, but it is important to bear this concept in mind when writing the entire research report.

Different criteria have been developed to articulate what makes qualitative research strong across the varying traditions of inquiry (e.g., Elliott, Fischer, & Rennie, 1999; Guba & Lincoln, 2005; Levitt, 2015; Maxwell, 1992; Morrow, 2005; Parker, 2004; Wertz et al., 2011; Williams & Morrow, 2009). Also, other authors have produced excellent guidelines for conducting and reviewing qualitative research that outline desirable features of single methods (Fassinger, 2005; Fine, 2013; Gilligan, 2015; Hill, 2012; Hoshmand, 2005; Kidd & Kral, 2005; Suzuki, Ahluwalia, Mattis, & Quizon, 2005; Wertz, 2005). These criteria often focus on identifying procedures that are advantageous to qualitative research. Although this approach can be helpful in the process of study design and

http://dx.doi.org/10.1037/0000121-003
Reporting Qualitative Research in Psychology: How to Meet APA Style Journal Article Reporting Standards, by H. M. Levitt

review, there are two central limitations. First, some qualitative researchers do not use established methods in their designs. They may pragmatically develop new methods to solve problems they are facing. Second, researchers who use established methods often adapt them to better address their questions, their topic, or other research study characteristics, and procedures that are useful in one context may be problematic in another. Because of this concern, there has been an interest in guidelines for evaluating qualitative studies that are not bound to specific sets of procedures but that articulate underlying principles. Understanding these principles and knowing how quality is judged will tell you what information you should report in your paper to enable that judgment.

When addressing methodological integrity,

- demonstrate that the claims made from the analysis are warranted. The procedures that support methodological integrity (i.e., fidelity and utility) typically are described across the relevant sections of a paper, but they could be addressed in a designated section when elaboration or emphasis would be helpful.

Trustworthiness and Methodological Integrity

The concept of *trustworthiness* was proposed to communicate the value of qualitative research and help consumers of research discern whether the claims made in a project are warranted (Lincoln & Guba, 1985; Morrow, 2005). This concept asserts that the evaluation of the worth of a qualitative research presentation should be based in the judgments of its readers. When publishing your findings, you want readers to trust that the findings are justified and that the procedures you selected merited such claims to be made. The idea of trustworthiness captures this sense and has been a valuable contribution to the field.

Building on this concept, the term *methodological integrity* has been advanced to identify the underlying methodological basis of trustworthiness (Levitt, Motulsky, Wertz, Morrow, & Ponterotto, 2017). Although the concept of trustworthiness gauges readers' faith in the project, it doesn't specify the grounds for that faith and may be based, in part, on features that are independent of the research design and execution. For instance, if your paper is in accord with biases and perspectives that your readers already hold, this might increase the trustworthiness of a paper for them. Or if a paper was penned by a famous psychologist, findings might be accepted more readily as trustworthy. In contrast, *methodological integrity* identifies the method-based evaluations that underlie trustworthiness. Methodological integrity does not focus on specific procedures that should be used in a project but rather on a contextualized rationale for selecting and adapting procedures on the basis of the features of individual research projects.

Instead of asserting that there is one correct way to conduct qualitative research, researchers are encouraged to consider how four elements of a study work in synergy together: (a) *Methods of analysis* and *research designs* (e.g., ethnography, conversational analysis) should be used in such a way that they (b) support the *research goals* (i.e., the research problems or questions); (c) are coherent within the researcher's *approaches to inquiry* (i.e., research traditions, including philosophical assumptions, worldview, and approach to problems); and (d) are adapted to fit the *study characteristics* at hand. In terms of study characteristics, researchers want to consider features related to the phenomenon under study (e.g., diversity and complexity within an experience or process), the investigators (e.g., whether an individual or team approach is best, relevant statuses or lived experiences), the research participants (e.g., how verbal and insightful they are, their potential to be engaged in research, their need for representation), and the resources available to support the research.

For instance, in a study on the development of researcher identities in graduate students, the investigators would want to report how their selection of methods relates to the goals of the project. Is the aim to provide a document to support students while in graduate school? Is the aim to influence university policy on what resources are needed in the formation of active research programs? Is the aim to inform instructors of graduate methods-related courses how to best foster enthusiasm for research? It may be that there are multiple goals, but it should be clear how the research methods were selected to best enable the study to meet its goals.

The methods selected should also make sense given the approach to inquiry. For instance, if the purpose is to articulate internal experiences of graduate students, a constructivist approach to inquiry would make sense. Researchers might interview students to learn how they construct their understanding of what it means to be a researcher and how their own questions and expectations relate to their answers. If, however, the approach is to change university systems, it might be useful to use a critical approach. Then, researchers might interview students but also professors and administrators to learn how people in different positions in the system might be misunderstanding one another's needs and values. The approach to inquiry, the methods, and the research goals all should be advancing one another.

In addition, the specific study characteristics might hold sway over what approaches to inquiry, methods, or goals are at play. For instance, it might be that researchers are unable to access financial information about students' scholarships. It might be that because the students are still in graduate school and just learning about research, many are still uncertain about their career goals, limiting the questions they can confidently answer. Maybe some who begin interested in applied work realize in time that they love research or vice versa. Maybe the position of researchers as people who know their participants limits the types of questions that can be asked. The qualities of the phenomenon explored, the characteristics of participants and investigators, and the resources available should all be considered in the design process.

Evaluation of Methodological Integrity

In contrast to approaches that evaluate methods on the basis of whether the researchers have adhered to fixed procedures associated with a given approach, methodological integrity can be understood as the evaluation of two components and their working together in the context of the study features as described in the preceding section. These two components are *fidelity to the subject matter* and *utility of research contributions*. Although fidelity and utility are at play throughout the research project and can be considered throughout the research endeavor (e.g., development of questions, literature review, discussion), I focus on their evaluation within data collection and analysis as these are central processes in the review of research design.

Both fidelity and utility can be assessed in reference to four features, which are discussed in turn (see Table 3.1). Although these features are not described in detail within the reporting standards, the standards are based on their conceptualization as described in Levitt, Motulsky, et al. (2017). These features may not all be reported in the Method section of a paper (indeed, their evaluation may occur throughout the paper). They are described here as well as in the final chapter of this book.

Table 3.1. Elements of Methodological Integrity and Reporting Standards

Feature	Evaluation of reporting	Examples of ways to report
Fidelity to the subject matter		
Adequate data for fidelity	Have you reported the ways you conceptualized and ensured that your data are adequate for your analysis?	Describe how your study adds to the understandings in the literature. Describe the features that might be most associated with diversity within your phenomenon and how your data encompass that diversity.
Perspective management in data collection	Have you reported how you managed the influence of your perspective in data collection?	Describe methods of evaluating and limiting how your perspective might influence data collection (e.g., memoing, bracketing). Describe using open-ended, nonleading questions. Describe seeking participant feedback on interview comprehensiveness. Describe seeking disconfirmation.
Perspective management in data analysis	Have you reported how you managed the influence of your perspective on the production of meaning in the analysis?	Describe how you evaluated and limited the influence of your perspective on the analysis (e.g., memoing, bracketing). Describe seeking participant feedback on findings. Describe methods of achieving consensus.
Groundedness	Have you demonstrated that your findings are grounded in the data?	Provide quotes and excerpts to illustrate the analytic process. Use compelling quotes and excerpts that bring the data to life.

▨ **Table 3.1.** (*Continued*)

Feature	Evaluation of reporting	Examples of ways to report
	Utility of contributions	
Contextualization	Have you presented your findings and data in a contextualized form and made their limits clear?	Provide contextual information for quoted or excerpted materials. Specify limitations of findings and the context of findings.
Catalyst for insight	Have you demonstrated how the study can lead to insights relevant to the project goals?	Articulate or demonstrate how the data collected are nuanced, detailed, reflective, or otherwise able to lead to insightful findings.
Meaning contributions	Have you described how the findings are meaningful contributions toward the project goal?	Establish the need for the research in relation to the literature reviewed in the introduction. Articulate in the discussion of findings how the findings advance research goals.
Coherence	Have you made clear how the meanings of findings are coherent with one another?	Articulate the relation among potentially discrepant findings so readers understand when and how differences occur. Discuss the implications of findings in a way that reflects on and integrates discrepant findings.

Fidelity to the Subject Matter

When reporting aspects of fidelity to the subject matter,

▪ assess the *adequacy* of the data in terms of the ability to capture forms of diversity most relevant to the question, research goals, and inquiry approach;

▪ describe how the *researchers' perspectives* were managed in both the data collection and analysis (e.g., to limit their effect on the data collection, to structure the analysis); and

▪ demonstrate that findings are *grounded* in the evidence (e.g., using quotes, excerpts, or descriptions of researchers' engagement in data collection).

As a qualitative researcher, you are concerned with fidelity throughout your study. Fidelity in reporting can be seen when researchers communicate that they selected procedures that develop and maintain allegiance to the phenomenon under study, as it is conceived within their approach to inquiry (e.g., the phenomenon might be understood as socially constructed). You seek to gather data and develop findings that will provide a clear and vivid portrayal or excerpt of the phenomenon you are studying. The concept of fidelity to the subject matter should be understood within the traditions or perspectives in use. For instance, you might understand your subject as a real phenomenon in the world (e.g., you might hold the experience of pain as an existential or biological given) or as a constructed phenomenon (e.g., you might think that the experience of pain is strongly influenced by learning, attention, and social convention). Even if you believe your phenomenon is constructed, you would still wish to collect data and develop findings that have a strong affinity to that experience and the processes of construction and interpretation, so that you can represent and describe the phenomenon cogently. Of the four features of fidelity, the first two, adequate data for fidelity and perspective management in data collection, focus on data collection, and the second two, perspective management in data analysis and groundedness, focus on the analytic process.

Adequate data for fidelity. When describing your data collection, you want to communicate information that will assure the reader that the data you have collected are adequate to capture the diversity features of your phenomenon most relevant to the question, research goals, and inquiry approach you are using (e.g., how people experience one event differently). Adequacy is evaluated in reference to the scope of the questions and goals you set. A case study of one participant might provide adequate diversity if it accords with your goal to expand on understandings of a phenomenon in the literature. Because it is not possible to obtain every type of diversity within an analysis, you would consider what types of diversity factors might be most likely to influence the experience you are studying and seek those out. For instance, if you are interested in Native American students' experiences of attending university, you might seek to gather data from students of different genders and ages and from different states who are studying a variety of subjects. If you are interested in Native American first-generation students' experiences of studying history, this question would shape the scope of factors that you would need to establish adequacy.

As you collect your data, your understanding of these factors might broaden, and you might deliberately seek participants who can help you better understand differences in your data (e.g., theoretical sampling; Glaser & Strauss, 1967). For instance, in your interviewing, you might discover that proximity to family is a characteristic that influences university experience and deliberately seek more participants who are living away from their families. Reporting clearly on how you established adequacy in your data collection gives readers confidence that your study can shed light on your phenomenon broadly.

Perspective management in data collection. Qualitative researchers tend to use a subjectivist rhetoric in which they are overt about the interpretive processes inherent in their research—that is, they seek to describe their perspectives when approaching and conducting the research. Describing your beliefs, values, identities, or positions can strengthen your research in two ways. First, it allows you to state how you sought to become aware of the ways your perspective might influence your research and to manage that influence. Second, it helps readers understand where you are coming from and your findings in that context. Although researchers might use their own perspectives to shape their question or decide on the purpose of their study, they seek to limit the influence of their own perspectives in the process of data collection as they want to hear participants' responses without biasing them. You want to report procedures you have used to manage your perspective, such as using open-ended questions and nonleading questions and evaluating your data collection design to limit or counterbalance your value commitments.

Perspective management in data analysis. When engaging in data analysis, qualitative researchers tend to use one of two strategies to manage their perspectives. Similar to perspective management in data collection, the first strategy is to attempt to limit the influence of your perspectives on the research project. You want to report whatever procedures you used to do this, such as an intensive engagement with the phenomenon that would broaden your understanding, use of multiple analysts to check one another's interpretations, use of participant feedback on your findings, and discussion of or memoing about your perspectives to check their influence on your analysis.

The second strategy is to actively use your perspectives to guide the analysis. For instance, researchers might interview women athletes in a study of sexism in university athletics. Because the researchers might have information about the ways men's athletics are financially supported of which participants might be unaware, and about how sexism evidences itself, they can use their knowledge to identify ways sexism is working that the participants themselves may not identify. This approach tends to be used in critical approaches to inquiry or in cases when researchers are interested in identifying trends or dynamics that participants might have trouble identifying (e.g., studying unconscious beliefs, studying patterns beyond participants' awareness or that of authors of texts under study). If you are using this strategy, you want to report on how you used your perspectives to structure the analysis and how they aided you in identifying results that could answer your questions.

Groundedness. Finally, you want to report in such a way that it is clear to readers that your findings are grounded in the data you have analyzed. Researchers often use quotes, excerpts, or descriptions of researchers' engagement in data collection to demonstrate the groundedness of their findings. Tying your interpretations to the data and showing how the analysis occurred increases readers' confidence in your findings, if you do this convincingly. This process is described at some length in Chapter 6, which focuses on the Results section.

Utility of Contributions

When reporting aspects of the utility of your contributions,

- demonstrate that the contributions are *insightful* and *meaningful* (e.g., in relation to the current literature and the study goal);
- provide relevant *contextual* information for findings (e.g., setting of study, information about participants, interview question asked is presented before excerpt as needed); and
- present findings in a *coherent* manner that makes sense of contradictions or disconfirming evidence in the data (e.g., reconcile discrepancies, describe why a conflict might exist in the findings).

The appropriateness of the data collection and analytic procedures that researchers select can be evaluated in terms of whether they strengthen the usefulness of the research contributions. In reporting, establishing utility is the process by which authors report whether they have selected procedures that usefully answer their research questions and address their aims. The aims of qualitative research can vary, and so the specific aims of the study need to be kept in mind (e.g., raising critical consciousness, developing theory, deepening understanding, identifying social practices, developing local knowledge). A study that produces findings that are useful in meeting its goals is a good study.

Whether findings are useful or not is judged in reference to a study's aims and tradition of inquiry. For instance, research conducted with a critical approach to inquiry should develop findings that can raise awareness of systemic processes of oppression and privilege. Research conducted to map out discursive patterns should contribute to the understanding of these social practices. And research conducted to aid clinical or educational activities should lead toward a richer understanding that can inform and enrich those practices. Four main features of utility are reviewed. The first two, contextualization and the catalyst for insight, are focused on data collection, and the latter two, meaningful contributions and coherence, are focused on data analysis.

Contextualization. Because qualitative researchers tend to study topics that are expected to shift across time, culture, and location, the data you present should be contextualized appropriately. When presenting quotes and findings, make clear their context, describe the questions that led to a response, or preface quotes or findings with contextual information. If you simply present a quote that says, "I could see that the male athletes were treated better and given more support," readers may wonder to which sport this quote was referring, the basis for the opinion, or the context of the participant. Context matters. It would help if you indicated that it was made by a senior college basketball player in reference to the discrepant number of scholarships provided for male players.

It is important to report the contextual information that can best situate the findings as well. It may be that what it means to be a female athlete in India or Sweden is quite different from what it means in the United States. Or it may be that holy texts in one era are translated in a manner that carries different meanings than in another era, producing conflicting analyses. Or it might be that the meaning of the homemaker social role in earlier generations is distinct from that in later generations. In all these cases, articulating the impact of context and how it might affect findings is key. It will not only allow your readers to understand your findings better but also assist them in transferring meanings to their own contexts.

Catalyst for insight. When describing your process of data collection or selection, you want to make evident to readers that your data were capable of leading to new understandings. Describing how you organized the data collection process to procure data that would be useful in responding to your study goal is central. This might entail providing evidence that the participants have a depth of knowledge or expertise about the phenomenon under study. Including justifications for texts or archives you have selected for your study can show readers why your data selection is appropriate.

You want to represent how your data source, you, and the relationship between the two can allow you to cull insights from data. For instance, it might be that young female athletes would feel uncomfortable disclosing their thoughts to senior male faculty. Or it might be that your participants are willing to reveal their genuine thoughts only to someone in the same community. Describe your relationship with your participants so that readers believe that your relationship would encourage insightful data rather than constrain their responses.

Meaningful contributions. Not only do the data have to promise insight, the findings of the research should also demonstrate that your findings actually do contribute to the literature. Again, whether or not something is a contribution would be judged in relation to your project goal, research tradition, and study characteristics, so you want to discuss your findings in relation to these aspects. This feature of utility is reviewed in more detail in Chapter 7 on the discussion of your findings.

Coherence. The final feature of utility describes the need to assist the reader in understanding findings that might, at first blush, seem to contradict or disconfirm other findings you present. You should present when or why data might indicate one situation in one instance and another situation later. Readers will not be able to make sense if you report that participants reported both liking and disliking hiring new graduates. It would be more useful to indicate that participants like hiring new graduates when they have more time to mentor but dislike hiring them when this time is unavailable. I often encourage students to consider the relationship between findings and see which fits best. It might be that usually X happens and rarely Y. Or that X happens only when Y occurs. Or that Y occurs only sometimes in the presence of X. You want to present your interpretation of patterns in your data to readers rather than having them need to guess at the implicit pattern.

Consistency.

> When addressing methodological integrity,
>
> ■ demonstrate *consistency* with regard to the analytic processes (e.g., analysts may use demonstrations of analyses to support consistency, describe their development of a stable perspective, interrater reliability, consensus) or describe responses to inconsistencies, as relevant (e.g., coders switching midanalysis, an interruption in the analytic process). If alterations in methodological integrity were made for ethical reasons, explicate those reasons and the adjustments made.

In addition to describing the use of procedures in relation to methodological integrity and its features, fidelity and utility, researchers need to make clear whether these procedures were used consistently or not. If you change the approaches and procedures you are using midanalysis, you want to describe why this occurred and how you dealt with the inconsistency. For instance, you might note that half the data were coded by two coders, but then one coder was unable to continue and a third coder stepped in. Efforts to establish consistency in spite of this disruption would be good to describe. Or if most data were collected at one time point and the rest at a later time, you would want to describe how this delay might have influenced your findings. Qualitative researchers tend to describe shifts in their own perspective across the research as another way of addressing the issue of consistency.

Comparing Fidelity and Utility

Although fidelity and utility may be intertwined, they are distinct concepts. For instance, imagine you are reading a study that sought to help students improve their study strategies, and you come across a qualitative study that carefully interviewed students and provided a beautiful portrayal of the nuances of the challenges in studying, with quotes that seem persuasive, insightful, and compelling. This study may have high fidelity, but if it didn't introduce you (or the literature) to any new study strategies, it has low utility. It might have helped you understand the problem, but the analysis produced only strategies that were obvious or commonly known, so it didn't meet its goal. You understand the problem better but have no better understanding of what students can do when the next test approaches.

Contrast that study with a similar interview study that provided many strategies students can try but did not present a good understanding of the problem or how the strategies helped students improve. The quotes are too brief to be meaningful, and the interviews appear superficial. You might see many things students can try, but you might doubt whether the strategies were really coming from a close understanding of the issues. This second study has low fidelity but higher utility. Although students can try the many strategies, you are unsure whether the strategies will be worthwhile, and you may be unsure how students can adapt the strategies to their own situation.

Ideally, a study has both high fidelity and high utility. Because the two ideas are intertwined, both fidelity and utility are increased if a study provides strong descriptions of the change process. Such a study would provide a clear understanding of the phenomenon and also meet the goals that it set out to accomplish.

Supplemental Checks on Methodological Integrity

When addressing methodological integrity, describe how support for claims was supplemented by any checks added to the qualitative analysis. Examples of supplemental checks that can strengthen the research may include

- transcripts/data collected returned to participants for feedback;
- triangulation across multiple sources of information, findings, or investigators;
- checks on the interview thoroughness or interviewer demands;
- consensus or auditing process;
- member checks or participant feedback on findings;
- data displays/matrices;
- in-depth thick description, case examples, illustrations;
- structured methods of researcher reflexivity (e.g., sending memos, field notes, diary, log books, journals, bracketing); or
- checks on the utility of findings in responding to the study problem (e.g., an evaluation of whether a solution worked).

Although the qualitative method itself is the central way rigor is established as it contains iterative analyses that encompass ongoing checks on an evolving analysis (Osbeck, 2014; Rennie, 2012; Wertz et al., 2011), researchers sometimes augment their analyses with supplemental checks. Examples of checks that researchers may wish to report to strengthen their analyses include the following:

- seeking participant feedback on the data collected or the findings of a study;
- using triangulation across multiple sources of information (e.g., participants and their spouses), findings (e.g., examining a question from two different angles), or investigators (having investigators code or analyze data separately and then compare their analyses);
- incorporating checks on interview thoroughness or interviewer demands (typically by asking participants whether they felt their interviews were complete or influenced by the interviewer);
- using a consensus or auditing process in which investigators both code and analyze the same data and consider one other's interpretations (consensus) or in which an investigator who has not coded a set of data reviews coding and analysis and provides feedback to be considered by the original coder (auditing);
- asking participants to provide feedback on findings;
- using data displays or matrices to vividly portray findings;
- presenting in-depth thick descriptions, case examples, or illustrations to bring findings to life;
- using structured methods to guide researcher reflexivity (e.g., memoing, field notes, diary, log book, journal, bracketing); and
- adding checks on the utility of findings in responding to the study problem (e.g., assessing whether a solution that arose in the findings actually works to address a problem).

Although all of these supplemental checks may be reported, it is rare that most of these checks are used in a given study. Approaches to inquiry tend to have sets of checks that they emphasize within their reporting traditions, and it can be useful to look at articles using the method or approach that you are using as models to help you make decisions. Also, in the process of designing your study, you want to consider what checks will be most useful in helping advance your research so that you can meet your study goals. This process will help limit the number of checks you need to report in the process of writing up your study.

Reporting on Methodological Integrity

Reporting on methodological integrity may include discrete sections that summarize strategies, but often it is dispersed throughout an article. For instance, Griffith (2016) explored how high-school–age youth developed trust with adults in the context of after-school programs. To demonstrate that she sought fidelity to her phenomenon, she described interviewing youth in a number of states and in different programs and asking them to draw graphs to indicate the trust development process from when they first met the adult until the present. The variation in youth, locations, and programs showed readers that she sought to collect rich and diverse data that included a breadth of examples and dynamics. The participants' graphs were presented in the article to document fidelity as well by showing a number of common trajectories.

To demonstrate the utility of her findings, Griffith (2016) described not only the average process of change but also various trajectories of trust development, and she identified critical processes within each. In this way, her findings had utility for a range of processes, identifying important issues for both youth with low initial trust and those with dips in trust over time that required repair. This close analysis increased utility by allowing readers to better use the findings in developing programs for youth with diverse patterns of trust.

Some authors include a subsection that conveys this information at the end of the Method section, where they highlight features of methodological integrity and related checks they have used. The following is an example of how my colleagues and I reported on the methodological integrity of a study (Levitt, Pomerville, & Surace, 2016):

Methodological Integrity Checks

Qualitative researchers often use processes such as consensus and auditor checks in order to enhance trustworthiness of findings (e.g., Levitt, Morrow, Motulsky, Ponterotto, & Wertz, 2016). These procedures demonstrate that an interpretation of data is shared by multiple people and is not idiosyncratic. We used four such checks.

1. Our team used consensus processes to enhance our sensitivity to multiple interpretations of data so that we could identify those that seemed to us the most meaningful representations. That is, rather than compete over interpretations, the authors attempted to understand each other's interpretations, discussed the rationales for those interpretations, and considered how interpretations might coexist (see Levitt, 2015, for a detailed description of their approach to consensus).
2. In grounded theory method, saturation is the point at which new incoming data stops leading to the development of new categories. This is the point at which data collection halts and the analysis is considered comprehensive. Saturation in this study occurred at the 47th study, meaning that the last 20 studies did not contribute new categories to the analysis—a high bar.
3. After an initial hierarchy was completed, the third author acted as an auditor to review the hierarchy and provide feedback on its representation of the data and its clarity. Feedback from the third author encouraged the team to clarify some of the category labels and also to pull together the lower-order categories related to clients' agency within the process of disengagement in one higher-order category. By reviewing the central findings within each cluster and considering them in relation to the findings across the hierarchy, the researchers developed principles to guide therapy (see Levitt et al., 2005, on this practice).
4. In addition to this check, a process of "fallible memoing" was used (Rennie, 1994). Fallible memoing is the effort to use note-taking to limit the influence of researchers' perspectives on the process of analysis, while holding that it is not possible to limit all researcher influence. The goal is to be open to the information in the data and also facilitate self-reflection. (p. 817)

Often this subsection draws attention to specific checks and allows readers to appreciate the efforts that were taken to establish the credibility of the findings.

When reporting your research, you want to make clear how your study had fidelity and utility overall. This reporting strategy of creating a section to summarize methodological integrity checks is useful both in alerting reviewers to the types of procedures that strengthened your research and in describing the function of any unusual research procedures you adapted to strengthen your study. Throughout your writing, the concept of methodological integrity can assist you in making decisions about what material is important to present so that reviewers and readers understand the logic behind your research design.

4

How to Situate Your Mission: Title Page, Abstract, and Introduction

At the beginning of every story, there are introductions. Characters are introduced. Their histories and backgrounds are explained. Their goals and problems are described. The tension of the story develops. As readers, we often care more about the story if we care about the people, the problems, and the issues in it. In the introduction of a research report, you are orienting readers by explaining why the question you are studying is important, so that they understand its ramifications. You are situating the story in your field so that readers can identify theories (and groups of theorists) that they follow and findings (or groups of researchers) on which they have relied. By doing this, you are helping build your readers' trust in your understanding of the subject in this process. You are helping them understand not only your mission but also how it moves forward the thinking and practices in your area of study. As readers come to understand the existing debates and the urgency of your problem, they will care about your study, and their curiosity about your study findings will increase.

Your description of the literature should be tailored to the readership of your story. A research article communicates a story to a very specific audience—scientists and research consumers. As you help them understand your paper as one that advances knowledge or solves a problem in a new way, you want your paper to speak using their language (typically measured, concise, and precise). Also, the audience will seek out your paper by searching their professional databases, so you want to help them locate your paper in the literature and determine whether it is relevant for them to read. The title page, abstract, and introduction of a paper are where this orientation usually occurs. For examples of the title, abstract, and keywords for 15 example articles, see the appendix at the end of the book.

http://dx.doi.org/10.1037/0000121-004

Reporting Qualitative Research in Psychology: How to Meet APA Style Journal Article Reporting Standards, by H. M. Levitt

Title Page

Title

> Your title should
>
> ■ identify the key issues/topic under consideration.

The title of an article communicates the key issues and topic on which a study is focused. Typically, it includes information about the phenomenon under study, the types of participants or data sources in use, and the context of the problem, and it should suggest the problem or question being engaged. You won't be able to include in the title everything that's important in your study. Because the *Publication Manual of the American Psychological Association* (6th ed.; American Psychological Association [APA], 2010, p. 23) recommends in Section 2.01 that titles have no more than 12 words (although some journals set higher limits), it can be challenging to include all of this information, and authors may need to decide what aspects are most central to their studies. Although sometimes researchers include in their titles the method of study, this is not necessary (just as quantitative researchers rarely indicate in their title the type of statistics they used in their analyses). Authors might wish to mention their method, though, when they want to draw attention to a methodological advancement in the field (as in a qualitative meta-analysis).

Good titles draw readers to an article because they clearly state what the paper is about. Imagine researchers sitting in front of a computer screen and searching for literature relevant to their project in an electronic database. They put into the system their search terms, and up come descriptions of hundreds of articles. They cannot read all of these articles. Instead, they search the titles for the articles that look most likely to contain the information they are seeking and then read the abstracts of those articles to narrow down which articles to read. You want your title to clearly communicate whether your article has the information they are seeking.

Catchy titles can compel readers to take notice of an article and check out what it is saying. Titles can incorporate metaphors, plays on words, and references to popular culture. An advantage of qualitative research is that the data often contain many evocative quotes that can be considered when forming a title. My favorite title from my own research was based on a direct quote from a study in which my coauthor and I analyzed interviews of religious leaders in the Mid-South region on issues related to domestic violence (Levitt & Ware, 2006). It captured their concerns about egalitarian marriages: "'Anything With Two Heads Is a Monster': Religious Leaders' Perspectives on Marital Equality and Domestic Violence." I still find this quote chilling.

As in this example, titles often include two parts, a main title followed by a colon and a subtitle. This format can help reduce the number of words in the title and make it more succinct. It is often tricky to fit all the information you might want in the title. For instance, I see that my title is a bit longer than the APA recommendation. If I needed to shorten the title, I might call the paper, "'Anything With Two Heads Is a Monster': Religious Leaders on Domestic Violence," as the focus of the larger project was on wife abuse. But I probably would remove the quote and call it "Religious Leaders' Perspectives on Marital Equality and Domestic Violence." Even though I like the quote, it isn't needed to help people search for and locate the paper—the main function of a title. It is unlikely that someone conducting a search on monsters will be interested in reading our paper! Because of the need to be succinct and to alert readers to the content of the article, you can see in the sample title pages provided in the appendix that many of the titles are very much to the point.

Author Note

Your author note should

- acknowledge funding sources or contributors, and
- acknowledge conflicts of interest, if any.

You may also thank people or agencies who provided support but were not authors.

Most papers include an author note. This note is useful in acknowledging funding sources or contributors who were not authors. For instance, graduate students often use this note to thank committee members who contributed to their dissertations by making editorial comments but did not contribute substantially enough to their papers to be listed as authors. Also, it is the place where authors report conflicts of interest, if they have any. Many papers do not include an author note, and there is no need for you to include one if you do not have this information to convey. Section 2.03 of the *Publication Manual* describes the typical components of an author note in more detail (APA, 2010, pp. 24–25).

Abstract

Your abstract should

- state the problem/question/objectives under investigation;
- indicate the study design, including types of participants or data sources, and analytic strategy, main results/findings, and main implications/significance; and
- identify five keywords.

Limited information will fit into your title, so the abstract gives you more space to summarize your study for potential readers to make decisions about its relevance to their purposes. The word limit typically ranges from 150 to 250 words, depending on the journal. Most journals provide online instructions for authors that specify this word count and other guidelines for formatting submissions.

An abstract typically identifies the main question or problem of your study, the salient characteristics of your data sources or participants, and relevant features of the study context (e.g., school, Southern United States, lower income neighborhood, medical hospital). It also provides a brief description of your method. Often researchers state their method of data collection and analysis, but they may wish to state their tradition of inquiry as well. Next, the abstract summarizes key findings and central implications of those findings.

The structure of the abstract reflects the key sections of a typical article. Although some journals ask that authors indicate the names of sections (e.g., Objectives, Method, Results, Conclusion) within their abstract, most do not, and so typically abstracts have more of a narrative flow consisting of a sentence or two from each of the main sections of your study. As stated in Section 2.04 of the *Publication Manual*, "A well-prepared abstract can be the most important single paragraph in an article" (APA, 2010, p. 26) because after the title, it is often the only point of contact readers will have with your article, potentially while browsing through multiple abstracts during a literature search. The *Publication Manual* elaborates that a well-written abstract is accurate, nonevaluative, coherent and readable, and concise. The appendix at the end of this book provides examples of good abstracts.

Typically, journals ask authors to identify three to five keywords, listed below the abstract, to help potential readers locate an article in electronic databases. For example, if I removed *marital equality* from the article title I described before, I still could list this term as a keyword to make it easier to find by readers interested in issues of equality. I might also include the keywords *religious leaders*, *domestic violence*, *intimate partner violence*, and *grounded theory*. In the Journal Article Reporting Standards for Qualitative Research (JARS–Qual), we recommend including at least one keyword that describes the method and one that describes the characteristics of participants or phenomena under investigation. To find standardized search terms, researchers may wish to consult the *Thesaurus of Psychological Index Terms* (Gallagher Tuleya, 2007) or examine the subject terms used in articles similar to their own. Examples of keywords are included in the appendix.

Public Significance Statement and Supplemental Materials

More recently, some journals have begun to request that authors provide a public significance statement for their work. These statements are intended to make clear to a nonprofessional audience the relevance of an article to the broader public. This audience could include practitioners, policymakers, patients, or media, so your statement should be written in accessible language and answer questions the audience might have. These statements are usually one to three sentences in length (about 30–70 words) and should be comprehensible without reference to the abstract or larger paper. An example is shown in Arczynski and Morrow's (2017) title page in the appendix.

Also, journals might make available the option to share supplemental material that is not necessary to understand the article but can enrich readers' understanding of a data set, procedure, or finding. The JARS–Qual Working Group recommends that journals permit an extra 10 pages for qualitative articles because of the length necessary to explain the methods used in qualitative analyses and to demonstrate the analytic process and findings via quoted materials. Instead of requiring all articles to adopt a standard length designed for quantitative manuscripts, the standards suggest that journals consider how to permit an adequate review process across distinctive methodological approaches. Still, articles describing qualitative studies may require more space, and the option of placing supplemental material online can be helpful so that nonintrinsic information can be shared in the review process and made available to readers. Examples of links to supplemental materials can be found in the title pages of two articles (Smith, Spiers, Simpson, & Nicholls, 2017; Suárez-Orozco et al., 2010) included in the appendix.

Introduction

There are two main elements in an introduction. The first is a review of the relevant literature, and the second is a description of the study's objectives. It is within these sections that you want to heighten readers' interest in your work. By organizing and relaying the story implicit in the literature in a clear and compelling manner, you invite readers to care about your work. Instead of having characters to develop, as in a novel, you engage readers by building their curiosity about your question and by familiarizing them with the debates that are resounding through a given field of study. In qualitative research, it is not uncommon to see writers draw on case examples, personal narratives, vignettes, or other illustrative material as a way to make clear the problem at hand and engage readers' curiosity. Section 2.05 in the *Publication Manual* suggests presenting the problem you are trying to solve and the ways your study approaches that problem to serve as the basis for a compelling story that will engage your readers (APA, 2010, p. 27).

Description of the Research Problem or Question: The Literature Review

The description of your research problem or question should

■ frame the problem or questions and the context and review, critique, and synthesize the applicable literature to identify key issues/debates/theoretical frameworks in the relevant literature to make clear barriers, knowledge gaps, or practical needs.

The goal of the description of your research problem or question is to place the problem or question under consideration in the context of the existing research on that topic and show how your study can advance the field. There are a number of ways to demonstrate that your work is a contribution to existing knowledge. Typically, a paper states clearly its central question and its context within the first couple of manuscript pages and then revisits this question in detail toward the end of the introduction when the study objectives can be reexamined in light of the literature review.

When writing papers for publication, it is the author's job to present the literature in a way that is easy for readers to digest so they can see the need for the current work. A strong introduction not only reviews theoretical writings and empirical studies but also organizes that information for readers in order to highlight common themes in the literature. Situating your work in terms of both its theoretical context and its relationship to prior empirical findings makes the value of your work clearer. When I engage in this process, I identify articles that are relevant to my topic, and then I develop a plan to organize the articles into sections and paragraphs to be described. Although I now usually work on a computer, I used to do this work sitting on the floor surrounded by piles of articles, shifting them from one pile to the next until a scheme formed. I continued to do this until I had a sense of how best to cast the story contained in the literature so that the plotline would demonstrate clearly the need for my own work.

There are a variety of ways to do this. Depending on the study, articles might best be grouped by the questions they ask, by their theoretical perspectives, by the types of participants and data sources, by their findings, by their methods, or chronologically by time period. The question is how well a method of organization will help contextualize your study and show that it is needed. There might be two levels of organization—perhaps sections of your introduction will focus on questions that have been asked, and then each paragraph within those sections will articulate the central trend running through the findings of those studies. Developing an outline (or multiple outlines) can help you compare alternative structures.

Once the literature is organized, it is easier to review groups of articles at a time and summarize their findings. It also becomes easier to identify and critique the literature in order to make clear where there have been barriers to further understanding, unrealized practical needs, or knowledge gaps that your study can remedy. Identifying these missing elements in the literature and showing how you can address them is the main function of your introduction. It tells readers what your work can offer. And by making clear what the needs are, you can set your study up to rush in and save the day as you shift to describe your study objectives.

Study Objectives

Your objectives description should

- state the purpose(s)/goal(s)/aim(s) of the study;
- state the target audience, if specific;
- provide the rationale for fit of design used to investigate this purpose/goal (e.g., theory building, explanatory, developing understanding, social action, description, highlighting social practices); and
- describe the approach to inquiry, if it illuminates the objectives and research rationale (e.g., descriptive, interpretive, feminist, psychoanalytic, postpositivist, constructivist, critical, postmodern or constructivist, or pragmatic approaches).

Usually the description of study objectives is relatively short—typically under a page. This description may be combined with the introduction or set off by a subheading. At this point, having reviewed the literature, you want to describe your objectives for the study in light of the issues and concerns you identified. In contrast to a quantitative study, you would not state specific hypotheses to be tested, as qualitative studies tend to be centrally inductive rather than deductive, but instead you would describe your research questions and goals. For instance, your goal might be to understand the experience of recovering from skin cancer or to examine the way competing discourses in the media have evolved in relation to birth control. If you intend your article to be read by a specific group of people, you want to state your target audience (e.g., mental health practitioners, teachers, physicians).

Also, in the objectives section, you want to describe the rationale for the methodological design you have selected and explain why it is appropriate for investigating your question. Because qualitative methods are still new for many audiences, you may need to make clear in a sentence or two how your method fits with your project. You would not have space in this section to describe what qualitative methods are as a whole or how they function; rather, you want to focus on the methodological choices you have made and how they correspond to the goal of your specific study.

For example, you might have selected a phenomenological approach to uncover the experiences of certain types of challenging psychotherapy clients because that method focuses on developing descriptions of internal lived experiences and might provide a deeper understanding of their experiences. Or you might have conducted a discourse analysis on how a political issue is being relayed in the media as a way to understand public sentiment because that method is designed to identify patterns in social communications. If it illuminates your objectives and your rationale for your design, you also might describe the approach to inquiry you are adopting. Indicating that you are working within a critical constructivist perspective, for instance, orients readers to the purpose of your study and how you understand your role as a researcher.

If your research has stemmed from a larger study, the description of objectives is the place to make this clear. Qualitative studies often legitimately need to be divided into multiple manuscripts because otherwise they would exceed journal page limits. This occurs when more explanation is required because readers are less familiar with qualitative methods and when methods are idiosyncratically adapted to fit a problem at hand so the method section needs to provide detailed descriptions of procedures and rationales. Results sections tend to be lengthy, too, because they are enhanced when authors provide excerpts from their raw data that illustrate how they developed their findings.

Even though dividing qualitative projects into multiple manuscripts is common, it is still incumbent on you to indicate how the current paper has a distinct objective and relevant literature that is under review. Also, you want to show that the current paper presents results and implications that are distinctive from other papers emanating from the same data. You want to communicate that your research has something unique to contribute. If helpful, you may begin to describe your own background and beliefs as a researcher (or team of researchers) as they relate to your study goal. Once you have articulated the context and focus of your investigation, readers will be expecting to hear how you developed your study design to carry out these intentions.

5

How to Describe Your Inquiry Process: The Method Section

Whether fiction or nonfiction, a good story is one in which the plot has a logic sustaining it. The type of logic will depend on the story, but an internal consistency often is required for a story to be believable. In describing the scientific quest, the way you have structured the quest and the choices you have made will be central to the faith readers will have in your findings. In your report, a logic should run through the way you framed your questions, the way you collected data, the methods and procedures you selected, and the ways you reached conclusions from that process. You will develop this logic throughout your paper, but you will focus on it most sharply in your Method section. Although often this section is thought to be a description of "what you did," I think it is better thought of as describing "what you did and why that made sense." Because qualitative methods and epistemologies are less familiar to many readers than quantitative approaches, the rationale for your choices is important to communicate.

I used to play a game with my kids when they were 4 and 6 years old called "Could It Happen?" I would give them a sentence, and they would say whether it could occur. For instance, I might say, "I went to the island." They would think about it and concede that this could happen. Then I would say, "I walked from here to the island." "No!" They would squeal. "You would have to swim!" Or I might say, "I read a book in the basement about the ghosts of Boston." They would agree this was likely enough. But then I would add, "I climbed a ladder up to the basement, and then I read a book about ghosts." "Couldn't happen!" they would say. "You have to go down to get to a basement!" They tried to identify the factor that weakened their confidence in my statement.

When writing an article, your reviewers and readers are interested in understanding not only what you did but also how plausible it is that what you did could lead

http://dx.doi.org/10.1037/0000121-005
Reporting Qualitative Research in Psychology: How to Meet APA Style Journal Article Reporting Standards, by H. M. Levitt

to findings in which they would have confidence. As an author, it will benefit you to consider what aspects of your study might weaken readers' confidence in your findings so you can address them in advance. Playing a version of the "Could It Happen?" game using the perspectives of various readers can help.

For instance, if you are interested in people's experience of divorce and you interview people who are married, will learning about not divorcing help you learn about divorcing? How likely is it that people who are married will really understand the experience of divorce and what it entails? How closely would their guesses about what it would mean reflect how they might really respond? How much confidence would you have in their answers compared with the answers of people who have lived through this experience?

I've seen this design, in which people are asked to describe an experience they did not have, used multiple times. Your readers may not have confidence that your study design will allow you to capture the real divorce experience. Married participants might be able to convey the experience of being married, a part of which might be to fear divorce, but they can't describe a divorce experience they have never had. It just isn't plausible. But if you report that all of your married participants had experienced a divorce before their current marriage, this qualification would strengthen readers' confidence in your findings. You are making clear that your method has integrity. It could happen that they can report accurately on a divorce experience.

The Method section is the part of your research story in which you lay out the terms of your adventure. What did you set out to do, and how and why did you set out to follow that course of action? You want your readers to understand what you did and to believe that the method you chose has led to findings that they can trust. To increase your readers' confidence, you want to do three things in the Method section: (a) be transparent in stating what you have done, (b) provide a rationale for your decisions, and (c) make evident the steps you took to enhance the methodological integrity of your study. In this chapter, I review the items that you might have in your Method section to help you be thorough in presenting your work, as noted in the Journal Article Reporting Standards for Qualitative Research (JARS–Qual; Levitt, Bamberg, et al., 2018). Although the Method section described in Section 2.06 of the *Publication Manual of the American Psychological Association* (6th ed.; American Psychological Association [APA], 2010) provides helpful suggestions for many research studies, it was not developed with an eye toward qualitative research methods, and JARS–Qual can help here.

Although I will review the Method section by indicating subsections that you might include, it may be that some subsections are not relevant to your project. You may find also that some elements of your design are relevant to multiple sections, and you will want to determine where to place them to describe your method coherently but reduce redundancy in your paper. Also, authors in some qualitative traditions tend to combine sections or to write Method sections in a chronological or narrative format. For instance, in some traditions (e.g., ethnography), the data collection and analysis can be intertwined (e.g., the data collection may be informed by ongoing analysis of the data), and it may make sense to combine these sections. It can be helpful to consult the journal you are considering submitting to to assess the format used for similar articles. In any case, the key is to ensure that the information needed to assess your method is present and clear. Also, because qualitative procedures may be creatively adapted and combined for use in individual projects, they require detailed description, and so qualitative Method sections tend to be longer than typical quantitative Method sections.

Another important distinction between qualitative and quantitative methods is that although you want to provide a method description that other investigators could follow, in most approaches to qualitative research it is not expected that others who use the same method as you describe would reach identical findings to those that you have developed. For instance, one research team may find that a therapy interaction was characterized by a poor therapeutic alliance, and another team may find, using the same method, that the same therapy was characterized by poor ethics. Both findings may be equally applicable in representing the dynamic at hand, and the differences do not undermine either finding. Indeed, both poor alliance and ethics may be at play, and the teams may elect distinctive emphases because of the issues of most relevance in their own perspectives or contexts. There is the expectation, however, that both studies should lead the teams to conclusions with a similar degree of methodological integrity.

Another reason that replicability is not a typical standard for qualitative research is that along with a strong drive to maintain fidelity to their data, most qualitative researchers apply processes of description and interpretation to subjects that they see as historically bound. They recognize that researchers bring to their research sets of questions, skills, and perspectives that can vary across place and time. A research team studying the meaning of water in one region of the world (e.g., the Sahara), for instance, would be expected to find different patterns in the data than a research team studying the same subject in Venice. Although the methods of both teams might be strong, their findings would not be identical. The phenomenon under study may have characteristics unique to a specific location, dynamic, group norm, and time period and might not be expected to replicate in a new context.

Research Design Overview

In your research design overview,

- summarize the research design: data collection strategies, data analytic strategies, and, if illuminating, approaches to inquiry (e.g., descriptive, interpretive, feminist, psychoanalytic, postpositivist, critical, postmodern or constructivist, pragmatic approaches) and
- provide the rationale for the design selected.

Let's say that you interviewed graduate students on their experience of developing a researcher identity, analyzed the data, and now want to describe it in your Method section. Often researchers begin their Method section with a paragraph that reviews their research design (i.e., their processes of data collection and analysis and their inquiry tradition, if illuminating). It foreshadows the subsections to come in the Method section.

If it is not clear already in the research objectives section, you might also include a sentence to provide the rationale for the design selected. At this point you would be brief. In the researcher identity study I described, you might just say that you interviewed graduate students about their developing researcher identities in your specific field and that you used a certain method (e.g., theme analysis, grounded theory, phenomenology) and inquiry tradition (e.g., constructivist, feminist, critical) to analyze the data. Academic writers strive to be concise, so you don't want to provide details here as they will come forth in the following subsections. This paragraph is just an orientation to what will come.

Study Participants or Data Sources

When writing a qualitative study, an understanding of who the participants were or where the data originated contextualizes the data that have been collected. There are many levels of contextualization that can be important to consider. For example, were your participants students from a certain state, city, school, grade, class, subject, age, or cultural background? In addition, you want to describe who you are as a researcher coming to the study and what your relationship is to your data sources, if there is any. Are you a teacher in that school, a textbook author, or a parent? The various ways that your participants' and your own perspectives might influence your study should be disclosed. You can determine the order of what you would like to present. Some researchers organize the subsection chronologically and begin with how they developed an interest in their study topic, whereas others begin by describing their participants.

Researcher Description

Within your description of the researchers in your study,

- describe the researchers' backgrounds in approaching the study, emphasizing their prior understandings of the phenomena under study (e.g., interviewers, analysts, or research team) and
- describe how prior understandings of the phenomena under study were managed and/or influenced the research (e.g., enhancing, limiting, or structuring data collection and analysis).

The question you are answering in the researcher description is how you came to be conducting this study and the perspectives on the topic you held as you began. You will not provide your life story in this subsection (or a list of your professional credentials), but you want to select information that makes transparent your prior understandings of the phenomena under study. This information might include (but is not limited to) descriptions of your demographic and cultural background, your credentials, your personal experience with the phenomena, any training you have had, your value commitments, and the decisions you made in selecting archives or material to analyze.

For instance, if you are running a comparative study on two treatment centers and you are employed by one of the centers, that would be important to mention. If you are conducting a study on immigrants, you may want to describe your own immigration status. Or if you are conducting a study on psychotherapy with a certain population, you want to describe your own psychotherapy orientation and your level of experience working with that population. Did you begin the study with certain beliefs and expectations? These factors are ones that may influence your perspective through your analysis and should be made explicit.

Your lived experiences can assist you in the analysis by allowing you to approach your study with greater sensitivity, or they can foreclose your thinking in directions than run counter to your experiences. Describe how prior understandings of the phenomena under study were managed or influenced the research (e.g., enhancing, limiting, or structuring data collection and analysis). If you are working with others (e.g., interviewers, analysts, research team), you want to provide this description of factors that might influence their perspective as well. Qualitative researchers hold an ethic of transparency in reporting their research, and readers will be looking to understand not only your prior commitments and beliefs as you began your study but also how you dealt with these in the course of your study. This description should include how those perspectives were managed and how they influenced the research.

For instance, if you were conducting the study in which you interviewed graduate students in your field on their development of a researcher identity, you may self-reflect and find that you are a keen researcher who is excited about the thrill of discovery and enjoys the process of learning from others about their experiences. You might describe how that attitude enhanced your work in some ways (maybe making you more sensitive to the descriptions of others' excitement) and limited it in others (maybe making it harder for you to understand why others would not enjoy research) and how you used your perspectives to aid you in structuring a process of data collection and analysis that would be sensitive to your topic (maybe deciding to adopt an attitude of curiosity to understand attitudes that differed from your own). Some researchers use procedures to help them reflexively consider their own perspectives (e.g., journaling, memoing, field notes) and work to limit their influence on the research (maybe being cautious to ask open-ended and nonleading questions, especially when opinions differ from their own) or best use those perspectives. Maybe, after getting a description of how your participants feel about research and recognizing the differences between their attitudes and yours, you might ask them what they think prevents them from experiencing excitement and thrill when doing research or what might help them do so. Whatever procedures you have used, you want to describe them.

An example of a description of researcher reflexivity from a study examining the complexities of power within feminist psychotherapy supervision is as follows:

Feminist–constructivist researchers situate themselves in the subject under study to assist the readers in drawing their own conclusions as to the influence of a researcher's views and social locations on the outcomes of research (Morrow, 2005). Both authors provide FM [feminist–multicultural] and social justice–oriented supervision and specialize in qualitative research focused on gender, diversity, and social justice. The first author is a non-Latino/a, White, English speaking, queer-identified in both gender and sexual orientation, first generation U.S. citizen, Polish American, feminist, early career university professor in counseling psychology.

The first author collected and analyzed the data with consultation from the second researcher. The second author was a non-Latina, White, English-speaking, cis-gender lesbian feminist, advanced career university professor in counseling psychology. She reviewed and provided feedback on data collection, analytic procedures, emergent framework, and drafts. Prior to data collection, we assumed that FM supervisors (a) are mindful of evaluation power, institutional power, and systems of oppression and privilege; (b) take action to not abuse their power; (c) place behavior into a lens of coping and resistance to oppression; and (d) facilitate integrating intrapsychic, interpersonal, socio/political, individual, familial, and cultural dimensions into client conceptualizations (Kulpinski, 2006; Nelson et al., 2006; Porter, 1995; Prouty, 1996).

I used several strategies to conduct a rigorous and credible analysis that was authentic to the participants' lived realities (Guba & Lincoln, 1989). In a reflexive journal, I notated my thoughts, emotions, and assumptions through-out the life of the project (Morrow, 2005). To refine the emerging framework, I maintained biweekly peer debriefing with colleagues and the second author to obtain feedback on study procedures, processes, and analyses as well as researcher biases and assumptions. I sought disconfirming evidence via follow-up and feedback interviews and peer debriefing in order to challenge confirmation bias and to add variation to the framework. I used an audit trail (i.e., a detailed chronology of the research tasks) to monitor implementation of rigor criteria, and I shared the de-identified audit trail with a panel of auditors. (Arczynski & Morrow, 2017, p. 4)

You can see in the example not only a description of the researchers' identities but a reflection on their assumptions at the beginning of their study and information on how they dealt with those assumptions. In other methods, such as critical approaches and task analysis, the researchers may use theoretical models to guide their analysis and may present in the text a description of the theory (e.g., critical race theory, feminist theory, queer theory) or the initial model they held (e.g., Pascual-Leone & Greenberg, 2007). More on this issue is given in Chapter 3 on methodological integrity.

Participants or Other Data Sources

In describing your participants or other data sources,

- provide the numbers of participants/documents/events analyzed;
- describe the demographics/cultural information, perspectives of participants, or characteristics of data sources that might influence the data collected;
- describe existing data sources, if relevant (e.g., newspapers, Internet, archive);
- provide data repository information for openly shared data, if applicable; and
- describe archival searches or process of locating data for analyses, if applicable.

In the subsection, you want to provide information about your participants or data sources. This may include the numbers of participants, documents, or events you analyzed. If you are working with participants, you also should include their relevant demographic and cultural information and factors that might have influenced their perspectives on the topic under study. You want to consider other descriptive features that might be relevant to your topic. The *Publication Manual* recommends that you "describe the [participants] as specifically as possible, with particular emphasis on characteristics that may have bearing on the interpretation of results" (APA, 2010, p. 29). For instance, in the study on asking graduate students about their developing researcher identities, you might want to ask the graduate students about their career goals and their training program focus.

If your study is not based on interviews but rather is focused on analyzing texts or other communications, you want to describe those data sources (e.g., newspapers, archives, Internet data) and any characteristics of the sources that might influence the data collected. Also, as applicable, you should provide data repository information for openly shared data and describe archival searches or processes of locating data for analyses. An example of this description can be found in Chang and Berk's (2009) study on clients' experience of cross-racial therapy:

The broad recruitment effort yielded a demographically diverse sample of participants, which is reflected in the demographic diversity of the 16 participants analyzed for this study. For this sample, ages ranged from 19 years to 50 years, with a mean of 33.5 (*SD* = 8.8). Highest educational level was mixed, with 5 participants who possessed advanced degrees, 2 who possessed an undergraduate degree, 6 who completed some college, and 3 who completed high school only. Five (32%) participants were born outside of the United States. Sexual orientation was not systematically assessed across the entire sample, although 6 (38%) participants self-identified as lesbian, gay, transgender, bisexual, or queer in the interview. All participants saw non-Hispanic White therapists, and 12 of the 16 therapists seen were female. Length of treatment ranged from 6 weeks to 6 years. Seven participants remained in therapy for 1 year or more, 7 remained in therapy for 6 months to a year, and 2 were treated for less than 6 months.

The most common presenting problems (not mutually exclusive) were "loneliness/isolating myself from other people" (9), "mood swings or depression" (9), "career/work-related stress" (9), "family conflicts" (8), and "feeling anxious for either known or unknown reasons" (5). Seven participants (44%) discussed their presenting problems in the context of racial or cultural issues. For example, two of the Asian clients described feeling resentment toward their families because they believed that childhood traumas they had suffered were exacerbated by cultural norms around gender and family roles. Several participants perceived discrimination from superiors and peers in school and in the workplace, which precipitated their distress and anxiety. Two immigrant clients also reported varying degrees of acculturative stress and experiences of prejudice and discrimination.

The majority of participants (9) saw therapists in a private practice setting, although 7 were treated in a clinic or hospital. There were no marked differences between clients who were satisfied and those who were dissatisfied with treatment with regard to age, treatment setting, duration of treatment, or presenting problem. The only characteristic that varied between groups was educational level: Everyone in the unsatisfied group had attended at least some college, whereas 3 of the participants in the satisfied group had graduated from high school only. (p. 524)

This example presents cultural information about the clients but also information about their therapy experiences and the context of their treatments that is relevant in the interpretation of the findings. As is often done in qualitative studies, the researchers also presented this information in a table to help readers appreciate the diversity of the participants. All of this information can help readers assess how likely it is that the findings would transfer to their own settings.

Researcher–Participant Relationship

When there are preexisting relationships between participants and researchers,

■ describe the relationships and interactions between researchers and participants relevant to the research process and any impact on the research process (e.g., whether there was a relationship prior to the research, whether there are any ethical considerations relevant to prior relationships).

Like your perspectives, your relationships with participants can be an advantage or disadvantage in qualitative research. If you have a prior relationship or a history of interacting with any of your participants, you want to describe its relevance to your research process and any impact on the process. For instance, in the researcher identity study, knowing some of the graduate students might help them feel comfortable confiding in you or, depending on your relationship, might hinder their confidence, and you would need to describe how you dealt with that. If you were an instructor or employer of the participants, how were ethical concerns around coercion addressed? If you were part of the community you studied, how did your involvement influence participants' willingness to participate and the data they provided? Answering these sorts of questions creates transparency and can help readers evaluate your work.

Participant Recruitment and Selection

The participant recruitment and selection subsection focuses on how you obtained participants. If you do not have participants in your study (e.g., if you're conducting arts-based text or communication analyses), you may wish to continue on to the subsection on data collection. Some studies begin by recruiting participants to the study and then select participants from the pool that responds. Other studies begin by selecting a type of participant pool and then recruit from within that pool. You want to order these subsections and their contents to reflect what you did in your study chronologically, whether that entailed selection or recruitment first.

Recruitment Process

In your description of your recruitment process,

- describe the recruitment process (e.g., face-to-face, telephone, mail, e-mail, recruitment protocols);
- describe any incentives or compensation, and provide assurance of relevant ethical processes of data collection and consent process as relevant (may include institutional review board approval, particular adaptations for vulnerable populations, safety monitoring);
- describe the process via which the number of participants was determined in relation to the study design;
- provide any changes in numbers through attrition and final number of participants/sources (if relevant, refusal rates or reasons for dropout);
- describe the rationale for a decision to halt data collection (e.g., saturation); and
- convey the study purpose as portrayed to participants, if different from the purpose stated.

How you recruited participants to make contact with you and join your study is of interest to readers. You want to describe the process you used to solicit participants (e.g., face-to-face, telephone, mail, e-mail, recruitment protocols, study descriptions). If you portrayed the purpose of your study to participants differently from the purpose stated in your research design overview, you want to make that clear, as well as your rationale for that difference. You may want to provide a rationale for the number of participants you included in your study, and typically this is established in relation to the method and tradition of inquiry you are using. Similarly, you should describe any procedure used that provided a rationale for your decision to halt data collection (e.g., adequacy, saturation; see Chapter 3, the section on Adequate Data for Fidelity, for more on adequacy, and Chapter 2, the section on Grounded Theory Approaches to Method, for more on saturation); justification for when the recruitment stopped can be presented in the subsection either on participant recruitment or on your analysis. If the number of participants in your study changed through the process of your study, you want to document any changes in the number of participants that occurred through attrition (as well as reasons for dropout) and clearly state the final number of participants or sources.

Keep in mind that there is no agreed-on minimum number of participants for a qualitative study. The number you use, however, should be understood in relation to your design and should allow you to adequately meet the goals of your study (see more on data adequacy in Chapter 3 on methodological integrity). Depending on how familiar the reviewers of the journal you are submitting to are with qualitative methods, you might add a statement to clarify how your number of participants fits with practices in the design you are using. Reviewers should recognize that transferability of findings in qualitative research to other contexts is based in developing deep and contextualized understandings that can be applied by readers and does not require the numbers of participants necessary for the statistical power needed to generalize from a sample. In other words, qualitative research is concerned with variability within a phenomenon under study rather than variability in samples and populations (Levitt, Motulsky, Wertz, Morrow, & Ponterotto, 2017).

Participant Selection

When describing the selection of participants,

- describe the participants/data sources selection process (e.g., purposive sampling methods such as maximum variation, diversity sampling; convenience sampling methods such as snowball selection, theoretical sampling) and inclusion/exclusion criteria;
- provide the general context for the study (when data were collected, sites of data collection); and
- if your participant selection is from an archived data set, describe the recruitment and selection process from that data set as well as any decisions in selecting sets of participants from that data set.

Whereas the recruitment process is how you brought people to become interested in your study, the participant selection process is how you decided whom to include. Some methods suggest sampling strategies that can be used to determine that number (e.g., theoretical sampling, diversity sampling), and if you used one of these sampling methods, you can tie the rationale to your design. In the participant selection subsection, you want to describe any participant selection processes you used. These might include purposive sampling methods (e.g., maximum variation sampling, theoretical sampling) or convenience sampling methods (e.g., snowball selection). Also, you want to list any inclusion and exclusion criteria.

Because the context of your participants often is a key factor in selection (e.g., they may all need to be in specific treatment, in schools, in a certain state), you want to identify the features of the context that are relevant for your study. In this process, you want to indicate when and where your data were collected or other features of participants' context that were important in selection. For example, the participants may have had to have a history of being in prison, even if they were not there currently.

Bowleg, Heckert, Brown, and Massie (2015), in a study on Black heterosexual men's discursive constructions of safer sex and masculinity, described processes of both recruitment and selection as follows:

> Participants were recruited from randomly selected venues (e.g., barbershops, street corners) in Philadelphia, Pennsylvania based on U.S. Census blocks with a Black population of at least 50%. Two Black male trained recruiters approached Black men who appeared to be at least 18 years old, and provided them with the study's recruitment postcard. The postcard invited men to participate in a confidential study about the "health and sexual experiences of Black men." Prospective participants were screened by phone to determine whether they met the study's eligibility criteria of: identifying as Black/African American, heterosexual, being between the ages of 18 and 44, and reporting vaginal sex in the past 2 months. After completing a brief self-administered demographic questionnaire, participants received a $50 cash incentive. . . . The Institutional Review Board of Drexel University, the first author's former institution, approved all study procedures. (p. 316)

This description first describes the context for recruitment and then describes how men were recruited who fit specific characteristics. In other studies, the order of these processes might be reversed.

Consent and Ethics

Whether your study design entails strategies of either participant recruitment or selection (or both), you want to state any incentives or compensation and provide assurance that ethical processes of data collection and consent were followed as relevant. Because the processes used in qualitative research can shift responsively as data are collected, the method might change as well. It might become evident that changes are needed in data collection, between collections, or between waves of collection. This means that ethics are not just considered at the beginning of a qualitative study but require consideration continually (see Haverkamp, 2005; Josselson, 2007).

These changes might not be predictable at the onset of a study. For instance, you might realize that your participants have had a more similar experience than expected, and to fully understand the scope of your question, you decide to recruit more strategically from within a set group of participants. It might be that your study on trauma leads you to focus on experiences of trauma that have various intensities or dimensions. Or you might realize that an approach to questioning that is less sensitive to the emotions of participants is needed. Sometimes data collection spans months or years, and you may learn things in one wave that lead you to alter your tack in a later wave.

You may wish to communicate to your institutional review board (IRB) that data collection may be narrowed or broadened within a certain scope or that questions may be altered between interviews. When writing your article, your readers will be interested to learn how ethics were managed, especially if you made decisions that will help them understand your methodological choices. This description may include reporting IRB approval and particular adaptations for vulnerable populations, such as safety monitoring. Chapter 1 of the *Publication Manual* provides more guidance on ethical and legal standards in publishing (APA, 2010, pp. 11–20).

Data Collection

In describing the aspects of data collection that are relevant to your study,

- state the form of data collected (e.g., interviews, questionnaires, media, observation);
- describe the origins or evolution of the data collection protocol;
- describe any alterations of data collection strategy in response to the evolving findings or the study rationale;
- describe the data selection or collection process (e.g., were others present when data were collected, number of times data were collected, duration of collection, context);
- convey the extensiveness of engagement (e.g., depth of engagement, time intensiveness of data collection);
- for interview and written studies, indicate the mean and range of the time duration in the data collection process (e.g., interviews were held for 75 to 110 minutes, with an average interview time of 90 minutes);
- describe the management or use of reflexivity in the data collection process, as it illuminates the study;
- describe the questions asked in data collection: content of central questions, form of the questions (e.g., open vs. closed); and
- identify data audio/visual recording methods, field notes, and transcription processes used.

Reviewers and readers will look in the data collection subsection to understand how data were obtained from your participants or data sources. Although I am referring to this process as *data collection*, you can use the terms for data collection that are coherent with your own research approach and process, such as data *identification*, *collection*, or *selection*. Descriptions should be provided, however, in accessible terms in relation to the readership. The questions you asked or the scheme for identifying data from a source are required. For data collections that include a long or varying list of questions, you do not need to report every question you ask (especially when presenting a series of unstructured or semistructured interviews in which questions are expected to be adjusted to the content of each interview), but you want to identify and convey the central questions. Also, it will help to identify whether the questions were designed to be open ended and nonleading or focused on a specific area. You want to describe the procedures you used to collect the data (e.g., interviews, questionnaires, observation) and any way that your procedures evolved through the course of your study, if at all.

For many qualitative methods, the questions asked are deliberately refined through the course of data collection as the researchers learn which questions lead to the most useful data, which questions are needed to provide a thorough understanding of the phenomenon, and what questions are needed to flesh out gaps in an evolving theory. You want to describe, along with the changes, your rationale for using them (see Josselson, 2013).

Details on the data collection process can help readers develop a sense of what the collection procedure was like. For instance, you might mention whether there were others present when observations occurred, the number of times data were collected, the duration of interviews, and their context. It would be a very different experience to be interviewed by your teacher in front of your class than to be interviewed by a stranger in a library setting or to be living in a community under study and collecting observations for a year. By providing this type of information on time intensiveness and extensiveness of your involvement as the researcher, you are also giving a sense of your depth of engagement in the data collection process. Descriptions of your engagement and your reflexive self-examination can help readers see not only that you obtained answers to questions you had but also how you increased your own sensitivity to better understand the meanings inherent in those answers. As part of describing the recording and data transformation process, you want to identify any recording methods used. Examples could include field notes, memos, audio recording, video recording, or transcription.

The following description of data collection in an interview-based study on the challenges of living with an ileostomy (Smith, Spiers, Simpson, & Nicholls, 2017) provides an example of data collection reporting:

> Interviews were undertaken by Johanna Spiers, either in person or via Skype/phone. We worked from an interview schedule which included questions on biography, illness, emotions, self and others. Here are the first three questions from our schedule to give the reader an idea of our interview style: (a) Can you tell me a bit about what the last few years have been like for you?; (b) When were you first told that you would need to have an ileostomy?; and (c) Can you tell me about going into the hospital to have the surgery? The full schedule is available as supplementary material online. The schedule was used flexibly in line with IPA [interpretative phenomenological analysis] good practice. The interviewer took opportunities to probe interesting and important issues which arose but these were those initiated by the participant rather than imposed by the interviewer.
>
> It has been suggested that telephone or Skype interviews may be detrimental to qualitative research as interviewers may miss body language cues and be unable to establish rapport. However, like several other scholars (Novick, 2008; Sturges & Hanrahan, 2004), we found no notable difference between phone/Skype and face to face interviews. Indeed, phone/Skype interviews may have been more convenient for some participants and allowed them greater freedom to discuss potentially difficult topics as the lack of face to face contact has the potential to give more of a sense of confidentiality (Smith, 1989). Interviews were audio recorded and transcribed verbatim; field notes were made afterward. Interviews lasted between 30 min and 130 min, most were 1 h. All data

have been anonymized to protect confidentiality. (Smith, Spiers, Simpson, & Nicholls, 2017, p. 144)

The following example of data collection from written texts is drawn from Rihacek and Danelova's (2016) analysis of written stories by therapists who had begun their training with one psychotherapy orientation but then developed an integrative psychotherapy orientation:

The contributors to Goldfried's book were asked by the editor "to narrate their growth experiences, illustrating the change process with anecdotes and illustrations" (Goldfried, 2005, p. x). They were asked to address five key aspects of their professional, as well as personal, evolution: (a) lessons originally learned, (b) strengths of original orientation, (c) limitations of original orientation, (d) how change occurred, and (e) current approach (for more detailed information, see Goldfried, 2005, pp. 14–15). The contributors to the issue of *Journal of Psychotherapy Integration*, dedicated to developmental journeys of integrative psychotherapists, were asked to reflect on their: (a) motivation, training, and development as integrative clinicians and researchers; (b) previous and current integrative practice and research; (c) future plans for integrative research and clinical/professional development; (d) goals, hopes, and predictions for the future of psychotherapy integration and the Society for the Exploration of Psychotherapy Integration (Lampropoulos, 2006b). The three stand-alone articles were presumably free of any unifying instructions. The length of the chapters and articles ranged from 8 to 26 pages, yielding over 400 pages of analyzed data altogether.

While it is more common in qualitative research to use interviews as a source of data, written accounts, such as diaries or autobiographic narratives, represent a viable alternative (e.g., Silverman, 2003) and have been used either as a stand-alone method of data collection (e.g., Gray & Lombardo, 2001; Pasupathi & Mansour, 2006) or in combination with other methods to enhance the validity of the study (e.g., Lawson, McClain, Matlock-Hetzel, Duffy, & Urbanovski, 1997; Topley, Schmelz, Henkenius-Kirschbaum, & Horvath, 2003). No direct empirical evaluation of the quality of data obtained from written narratives, as compared to interviews, has been found. Nevertheless, the use of written narratives can be supported by several arguments: (a) writing a narrative gives the author enough time to recall the details of their earlier experiences; (b) it lets participants develop their thoughts without being influenced by the researcher (Dahlberg et al., as cited in Persson & Friberg, 2009); (c) research on trauma memories suggests that writing, as opposed to spontaneous oral reports, helps participants organize components of their memory in a sequential fashion (Peace & Porter, 2004), which is particularly useful regarding the goal of this study; and (d) using published narratives gives the reader an opportunity to assess the authors' conceptualizations and interpretations. There are, of course, also several drawbacks regarding the analysis of writing: (a) it may be considered a barrier for those with poor writing skills (which was not the case in our study); (b) it deprives the researcher of the possibility to react to the participants and explore in depth aspects which were only briefly mentioned; (c) the narratives, especially if created for some another purpose, may not be fully focused on the research question; and (d) it gives the participants more space for stylization

N1 and may hinder the revelation of material that would be spontaneously presented within an interview. (p. 80)[1]

In both cases, the authors not only described what they did but also wisely provided justification for procedures that they anticipated might raise questions.

Analysis

Your analysis should include the following elements, as relevant:

- describe the method and procedures used and for what purpose/goal;
- explicate in detail the process of analysis, including some discussion of the procedures (e.g., coding, thematic analysis) with a principle of transparency;
- describe coders or analysts and their training, if not already described in the researcher description section (e.g., coder selection, collaboration groups);
- identify whether coding categories emerged from the analyses or were developed a priori;
- identify units of analysis (e.g., entire transcript, unit, text) and how units were formed, if applicable;
- describe the process of arriving at an analytic scheme, if applicable (e.g., if one was developed before or during the analysis or was emergent throughout);
- provide illustrations and descriptions of their development, if relevant; and
- indicate software, if used.

It is important to be specific in conveying your data analysis strategies. It is insufficient in most academic journals to simply say that you performed "a qualitative analysis." Although you don't need to use an established qualitative method (e.g., content analysis, consensual research, conversational analysis), it can be helpful as these methods often have developed reporting styles that can serve as models for you. In any case, though, you will need to describe each of the procedures you used in working with the data as well as provide a rationale for these steps so readers understand the purpose of your procedures. Typically, this description includes the units of analysis (e.g., entire transcript, speech turn, text entry) and how the units were formed (e.g., by how many readers?), if applicable. The description of the analysis process usually includes details about how categories of units were formed; how coding was conducted; how units, categories, text, or themes were labeled; how descriptions were formed; and how interpretations were made.

There are many approaches to qualitative research that have their own language for the procedures researchers use (e.g., axial coding, eidetic analysis, saturation). Using the language generated for your approach to describe your procedures is helpful in placing your work squarely within that tradition. It is important, though, to remember that unless you are publishing in a journal intended only for readers who have expertise in that method, you need to explain what the terms mean and the rationale

---

[1]From "The Journey of an Integrationist: A Grounded Theory Analysis," by T. Rihacek and E. Danelova, 2016, *Psychotherapy, 53,* p. 80. Copyright 2016 by the American Psychological Association.

for that procedure. That way, everyone reading your paper will understand what your method entailed.

Depending on whether you think it would be helpful for readers and whether you have space, you may provide examples of the way you worked with data to arrive at your finding. For instance, if you were conducting a phenomenological study, you might provide an example of a meaning unit. Or if you were conducting a conversational analysis, you might exemplify how you prepared your transcript for analysis (e.g., with signifiers of emphasis, volume, overlapping statements). The purpose of these examples is to help readers see how your analysis evolved and culminated in your findings. These demonstrations may be more important if you are publishing in a journal whose reviewers or readers are unfamiliar with qualitative methods.

The training and competence of coders or analysts should be described as well, if not already described in the researcher description section. For instance, you might say how the coders were selected (e.g., doctoral students in the lab, from a campus student group, from a community organization) and how the coding was conducted (e.g., in small groups that sought consensus, with two raters working toward interrater reliability, by a single rater who had an intensive engagement with the phenomenon).

You want to be clear whether any coding categories emerged from the analyses or were developed before the study began. If they were selected beforehand, then the rationale for that selection should be explained. If they emerged from the analysis, then you want to describe how that occurred. Illustrations and descriptions of the process of development and coding can be provided if they prove helpful. In addition, when indicated, the name of any software that was used should be provided, as well as its function. Although most qualitative software is simply an organizational tool, readers may misunderstand and think that the software is actually conducting the analysis itself.

The following description of an analysis of chronic illness narratives by Gomersall and Madill (2015) provides an example of a method that uses a theory-driven approach to discursive analysis:

> Transcripts were inspected for key moments defined as emotionally laden stories relevant to this original purpose which had a recognizable beginning and end. Hence, key moments can be viewed as distinct episodes within the overall narrative structure of the interview (see Madill & Sullivan, 2010). In total, 186 key moments were identified, ranging between a quarter page to just over two pages of A4 in length, with participants contributing between two and 12 key moments each. Key moments were initially analyzed in terms of the following categories that operationalize central features of Bakhtin's (1981, 1984) theory of chronotope: genre(s), emotional register, time–space elaboration, context. Notes pertaining to these four categories were written up into a table for each participant. While a variety of chronotopes were identified in the data (e.g., cyclical time, medical and lay timespaces), chronotope disruption was identified as an important phenomenon in that all participants described, in relation to their diabetes, increasing challenges in their embodied relationship with, or being in, time and space.
>
> Detailed familiarity with relevant key moments allowed us to identify three main patterns of chronotope disruption. We named each pattern in way that captured its central meaning. In the following section we provide an analysis of each identified pattern of chronotope disruption through close discursive analysis of

exemplar extracts paying particular attention to time-space elaboration and emotional register (see Sullivan, 2012). (p. 409)

In contrast, Shelton and Delgado-Romero's (2011) description of a phenomenological analysis of the experience of sexual orientation microaggressions provides an example of an analysis in which coding categories emerged from the analytic process:

> Preliminary data analysis was independently completed by the primary researcher. Responsibilities of the second researcher included providing feedback on the analysis, psychologically transformed labels, and complementariness of themes with transcribed statements. The analysis of this investigation was derived from the guidelines of Moustakas (1994) and the "Duquesne method," which involved (a) collecting verbal protocols that described the experience, (b) reading them through carefully to get a sense of the whole, (c) extracting significant statements, (d) eliminating irrelevant repetition, (e) identifying central themes, and (f) integrating these meanings into a single description (Creswell, 1998).
>
> The collection of verbal data from the focus groups began the process of exploring LGBQ psychotherapy clients' lived experiences of microaggressions. After the data were collected and transcribed, it was read in its entirety multiple times to gain a sense of the experiences of participants as a whole.
>
> Following a full depiction of participant experiences, the data were reduced into significant statements and descriptions that formed meaningful units. Creating units of meaning was done by reading and rereading the transcripts more slowly, and acknowledging a series of meaningful statements or shared ideas. Using the guidelines of the van Kaam method of phenomenological analysis (cited in Moustakas, 1994), statements that did not meet the following criteria were eliminated from the study: (a) statements that contained a moment of the experience that was sufficient for understanding it and (b) statements that could be abstracted and labeled.
>
> Meaningful units were then clustered together into central themes, and the essence of the phenomenon was described using the participants' language. Participants' language was then transformed into psychologically sensitive expressions (Giorgi, 2006); for example, the description of an experience that conveyed subtle discrimination was transformed into the psychological label of a microaggression. Completing the data analysis involved providing both a textual description (description of the participant's experience) and structural description (context in which microaggressions take place) from the synthesized and transformed data (Creswell, 1998; Creswell, Hanson, Clark, & Morales, 2007). (p. 213)

In addition, your analysis might be one in which you have used procedures that have stemmed from varying qualitative methods (e.g., Chang & Berk, 2009). In this case, you want to describe the procedures you have used and credit them appropriately.

How Much to Report

After reading this chapter and seeing all the aspects of methods that can be reported, you may find it a daunting task to write an article-length Method section. Because qualitative methods are so diverse and tend to be less well understood, qualitative Method sections tend to be longer than quantitative Method sections because they require a good deal of description. Although there is not a rule, I tend to aim for a 15-page double-spaced Method section in my first draft of a manuscript, and then I cut from there to meet a journal's page length requirements. Unfortunately, you will have to make choices at points on what you can present, and you may not be able to present all the information recommended here. You may need to decide whether to submit to a journal with a very restrictive page length (and not be able to present many of the methodological details or rich results) or to submit to a journal that allows more space. Fortunately, some journals (e.g., *Journal of Counseling Psychology*) are beginning to permit longer manuscripts for qualitative research in recognition of the need for more methodological detail (and lengthier results) in this form of research. Also, some journals permit materials to be hyperlinked to a database of supplemental online information and so details can be reproduced there. The instructions for authors on a journal's webpage usually provide guidance on these points.

It can be helpful to examine other qualitative research published in the journal to which you wish to submit your paper. This review may aid you in making decisions on the types of information that is valued in that journal and how familiar its reviewers and readers are with qualitative methods. If they are less familiar with qualitative methods, it may prompt you to provide more extensive description and to adapt your language so it is intelligible to their readership.

Still, even within a journal, reviewers can vary in their demands, and it can be challenging to anticipate what information they would like to receive. For instance, although some reviewers are not at all interested in hearing about authors' preconceptions, other journals expect pages to be written to situate the researchers at the beginning of the research and throughout its unfolding. Increasingly, reviewers understand that qualitative authors typically have to make choices about what to present and that it is challenging for them to predict what to include, given the varied expectations that have existed. So even if you have to abbreviate information from your manuscript when you submit it, you may have the opportunity to expand your reporting in a revision.

6

What Did You Find? The Results Section

Ihave to confess to loving writing qualitative results descriptions more than any other part of the manuscript. The Results section is where you finally get to share the findings you worked so hard to generate. This is the moment of the research in which discovery occurs and your tale reaches a climax. As in a mystery, this is where the clues come together and a new understanding is revealed. As in an adventure story, this is where the hero discovers the answers that open the doors to the kingdom. Readers have been reading along in wait for this description, building their anticipation. Although it can be a time-intensive and demanding task, I find that writing the Results section is a labor of love as qualitative research is such an engulfing task that I often feel quite enthusiastic about my findings by the time I am describing them. It is a privilege to be able to share with the world your understanding of a topic and to generate compelling ways of seeing it anew.

A strong Results section is a pleasure to read. Peppering your analysis with excerpts, notes, quotes, or illustrations, you paint for readers a picture of your phenomenon that can guide them to appreciate new aspects and envision it more completely then they had previously. Because the results bring to life the communications or experiences in your data, they are not dry and impersonal but tend to resonate with readers' personal histories. Because findings are deeply contextualized in participants' characteristics and interpersonal dynamics, they are readily transferable by clinicians, educators, advocates, or practitioners. Because the narrative arc follows changes across time, Results sections can have the appeal of a novel while maintaining the value of empirical research.

http://dx.doi.org/10.1037/0000121-006
Reporting Qualitative Research in Psychology: How to Meet APA Style Journal Article Reporting Standards, by H. M. Levitt

Depending on the approach to inquiry, a personalized discursive style might be used that portrays the researchers' involvement in the analysis. The Results section might read as a narrative that follows the investigators as they begin their analysis and develop an understanding of their phenomenon and, perhaps, find their own perspectives changing in the research process. Because of the emphasis on reflexive self-analysis to examine your interaction with the research process, the use of the first-person voice is much more common in qualitative than in quantitative papers.

There are ways of presenting your work that will enhance the presentation of your results. As discussed previously, qualitative researchers tend to present their research in varied ways. Some traditions combine the description of method and results into one section. This style of presentation tends to be used most often when the method changes responsively in relation to the results that are collected. Other traditions combine their description of the results with the discussion. Presentations in this form can be especially effective when the discussion of some findings leads to a deeper understanding of other findings.

In any case, you want to present your research in a way that is compatible with the study design you have used—and there may be multiple ways this can be accomplished when presenting your work to a given audience. Although I refer to the "Results section" in this chapter, most of the recommendations also apply when the results are intertwined with other sections (although the provisional template in Exhibit 6.1 would need to be adapted). In this chapter, I review the standards for reporting results and describe some practices that have helped my students learn how to present qualitative results for publication in social science journals.

Exhibit 6.1.

Provisional Template for Qualitative Results Sections

For teaching qualitative research classes, I developed a template to help students with the process of presenting qualitative research. (A version of this template is described in an article on how to publish qualitative research with a research methods class; Levitt, Kannan, & Ippolito, 2013.) This template is most useful for methods that focus on organizing data by conceptualizing commonalities and patterns, such as in phenomenology, content analysis, narrative analysis, consensual qualitative research, theme analysis, or grounded theory analysis. Although the template may not easily fit all methods, it may be adjusted to fit a wide variety of methods and so it is presented as a tentative guide.

It is always a good idea to look at Results sections of articles describing studies using methods similar to your own, within the same journal if possible. In this way, you can learn about similar traditions of research reporting and can compare this template to the presentation of findings in those articles to help you create an outline for presenting your results. By beginning with an outline of the sections and subsections in your article, you can plan the flow of your paper and its presentation. Then, when you begin writing, it is far less daunting a task.

▓ **Exhibit 6.1.** (*Continued*)

Orientation Paragraph

The initial, orientation paragraph is a conceptual overview of the study's findings and can describe their form (e.g., number of main findings, organizational structure of the findings). This paragraph can discuss issues related to the decision of when your analysis was completed (e.g., saturation). Also, if you use quantification in your Results section, you can describe here how to interpret those numbers when they are presented.

Section 1: Main Finding 1

You may find it helpful to organize the subsections in your Results section so that each reviews a main finding from your analysis. The first paragraph of the first subsection will contain a brief overview of the first finding. Consider the order of the findings you present so you can organize them in either a developmental or a logical sequence. Thinking about the organization of findings (and subfindings) in advance will help ensure that your description of the findings flows and redundancy is reduced. Readers need to have encountered in earlier sections the information needed to fully understand the Results section. In this paragraph, you might describe how many subfindings were developed, if your analysis included subfindings. If you are using quantification, you can include that information here as well.

Subsection 1

Subfindings may or may not be organized into paragraphs with subheadings, depending on the tradition you use and whether or not the description of findings is best aided by having a contiguous narrative format. In any case, you can use separate paragraphs to elaborate on the distinct ideas within each of the main findings. Sometimes this description can be accomplished in one paragraph, but at other times it might take a number of paragraphs. Each of the subfinding ideas is presented in such a way as to make clear the position of the component in relation to the larger finding. Typically, a quote or excerpt or two are presented to illustrate the finding. Remember to provide contextual information to help situate your quotes or excerpts. Then add a concluding sentence that ties the meaning of the quotes or excerpts back to the research question or the larger theme to make clear to readers what you found to be important about them in shedding light on your data.

Subsection 2

In Subsection 2, follow the instructions for Subsection 1 again and continue to follow the instructions for additional subsections.

(*exhibit continues*)

■ **Exhibit 6.1.** (*Continued*)

Section 2: Main Finding 2

For Section 2, follow the instructions for Section 1 again and continue to follow the instructions for additional sections.

Overarching Finding or Summary Paragraph

Some methods have overarching findings that are developed from the findings to summarize a main theme or a central organizing factor that runs across the findings. For instance, grounded theory analyses have core categories that are based on the examination of lower-level categories in a data hierarchy (e.g., Glaser & Strauss, 1967). Some authors place the central findings at the top of their Results section between the orientation paragraph and the description of the first main finding, and others prefer to place this finding at the end of the descriptions of main findings (as I have placed it here). Either way can work. I prefer to place central findings at the end of my Results section because then I can refer back to the concepts that I have described already in the other findings that this overarching finding is built on. This placement minimizes redundancy, and I find that it permits space for a richer discussion to occur. Also, then I can describe more efficiently how the main finding was drawn from the findings that were described previously so that it is clear how it was grounded in the analysis.

If there is not an overarching finding in the method or approach you are using that draws together a central meaning from your results (e.g., theme analyses tend to produce a list of findings that may answer multiple questions), it will be useful to end your Results section with a paragraph or two that summarize the themes and positions them in relation to one another. Think about this paragraph as guiding readers to develop a sharp understanding of what to take away from your paper. If someone asked them after reading your paper, "What did the authors find?" you hope that they would recite this paragraph. This paragraph can organize your findings so readers can better hold them in mind when moving on to read the Discussion section and consider the implications of your findings.

Describing and Demonstrating Your Analysis

In your Results section,

- describe research findings (e.g., themes, categories, narratives) and the meaning and understandings that the researcher has derived from the data analysis;
- demonstrate the analytic process of reaching findings (e.g., quotes, excerpts of data);
- present research findings in a way that is compatible with the study design; and
- present synthesizing illustrations (e.g., diagrams, tables, models), if useful in organizing and conveying findings. Photographs or links to videos can be used.

Your Results section presents your description or interpretation of your phenomenon rather than the texts, materials, or transcripts you analyzed. As a reviewer, I have read many papers in which the Results sections are heavy on quotes but weak on analysis. Even findings of studies using an artistic qualitative method (e.g., link to a dramatic presentation of findings) also require the clear presentation of findings, as indicated in the Qualitative Journal Article Reporting Standards, to support the research presentation. Focusing your Results section on exemplars of your data or artistic presentations and omitting your analysis of them may be appropriate for a creative nonfiction or arts journal but will not serve the purpose of articles in a scientific journal. These practices are not helpful as they leave the analytic work to readers, and readers rarely have access to the complete set of data and have not engaged in the analytic process.

The analysis is the job of the researcher. Readers want you to do the work of conducting and presenting your analysis, and although exemplars from your data are helpful to show how you derived findings, your analysis needs to be front and center. You are presenting your findings in the Results section, not raw data. As a consequence, findings should be organized by the central categories, themes, descriptions, or understandings developed in your analysis. Still, you want to exemplify your analysis within the presentation of your findings.

The need to present material to exemplify your work is the reason why qualitative Results sections tend to be longer than quantitative Results sections. Selecting material carefully can help in this process, but lengthy manuscripts are almost unavoidable because the assessment of aspects of methodological integrity (groundedness, contextualization, and coherence; see Chapter 3) depends on detailed description. As journals begin to recognize the value in not forcing qualitative research to meet page limits that were developed for quantitative research, they may make allowances that can improve research reporting and develop guidance for placing supplemental materials online. This space can benefit the field by allowing the methodological integrity of qualitative research to be more comprehensively evaluated.

Representing Processes Descriptively in Labeling of Findings

To maximize fidelity, the Results section should be clear in both the labeling and description of categories, themes, or other forms of qualitative findings. Strengths of qualitative research methods include their ability to identify underlying values or experiences that may be hard to articulate. For instance, in describing the effects of heterosexist stigma on same-sex relationships, Frost (2011) created a powerful category called "Stigma as Contamination" and another called "Stigma as Opportunity for (Re)Definition." He captured the central nature of the experience he was studying in a vivid manner. These categories are much stronger than ones such as "Types of Stigma" or "Stigma Affects Relationships," which do not convey the distinctive dynamics specific to same-sex relationships.

Findings and their labels also are strengthened when authors show processes as in flux and in relation to contextual factors as they convey findings. The length of the category title is not as important as its ability to describe your phenomenon in a useful manner. Indeed, it is advantageous for qualitative researchers to present findings in a manner that helps readers understand these features. For instance, "Children Prefer

Eating Unhealthy Food" is a category title with less methodological integrity than a title that specifies "In Contexts Where Fresh Produce Is Unavailable or Is Too Expensive, Children Prefer Eating Unhealthy Food." Qualifiers like this can help researchers better use the findings to reach their larger goals (e.g., developing health initiatives) and better describe their phenomenon.

I like to use the central category titles as headings in my Results sections, but this is not a requirement, and some journals may prefer you to use pithier versions of these labels when your category titles are longer for aesthetic reasons. The length and types of details provided in a finding should be considered in relation to the goals of your research. For instance, generating categories that are easy to recognize and code is important if you are conducting a qualitative study to generate a coding scale. Or, if your study is intended to guide the labeling of factors within a quantitative analysis, you would want to create categories with titles or labels that can help you achieve that goal. In any case, you want to form both the finding label and the finding description to best reach your study aims and maximize their utility.

Selecting Quotations or Excerpts

You want to demonstrate the analytic process to show readers how you came to your findings. They will have trust in your work if they can see the methodological integrity in your analyses. To do this, researchers can exemplify how their findings were based in quotes or excerpts of their data or by citing field notes, journal entries, or memos. They typically describe the finding that was produced by the analysis and then use thick description to show how the finding arose from that data, including exemplars that show a behavior in context and with reference to the intentionality of its actors and their thoughts and emotions (Ponterotto, 2006). Exemplars should be selected carefully to accomplish the following goals:

- *Avoid redundancy and deepen understanding of intentions, thoughts, and emotions.* Imagine reading a passage in a study on the meaning of candy for U.S. young adults that describes participants' zest for chocolate and then encountering this quote: "I just love chocolate. I really do! I think it is great." Although the quote does demonstrate that the finding was rooted in the data, it does not add any understanding to the description of the finding. It is also hard to tell from the quote whether this was a casual aside or a flippant or joking remark and the function of this preference. Instead, a quote that deepens readers' understanding, like the one presented next, is more valuable and strengthens the fidelity of your finding.
- *Use evocative description to convey findings.* For instance, consider the following quote:

> When I receive good chocolate, it makes me feel really cared for. It is something that is sensual but classically romantic. It focuses my attention inward and away from distractions as I linger and savor the creamy taste. Eating it with a mug of hot coffee or tea is the best because it melts in my mouth. Even if it is fleeting, it can create a moment of silence for me to just focus on my own pleasure, which can be hard to come by with all the pressures in my life. And it is especially romantic when you can share it with a partner and both see each other's enjoyment.

In addition to framing the speaker's intentions, emotions, thoughts, and interpersonal purposes around eating chocolate, this quote uses rich language that brings to life the experience of chocolate and helps readers understand more holistically its meaning.

■ *Select material that represents your finding.* If readers cannot see the connection between your exemplar and the finding you are presenting, the trustworthiness of your research will be weakened. The evocative quote above is not any good if your finding is that your participants loved candy but generally were neutral about chocolate, unless it is presented clearly as an exception and discussed as such. You want to be sure that the material you report represents your findings well.

Depending on the length of the manuscript, you will need to make decisions about how many exemplars you can use and their length. Although I usually prepare my initial manuscript draft so that it contains multiple exemplars for each finding I can select from as the paper takes shape, I find that I typically can provide about one longer exemplar (about two to four sentences) or two short exemplars (about one sentence each) for every main finding. In addition to quotes, field notes, memos, and text excerpts, you can use illustrations to synthesize your findings and make them more accessible for your readers (see Tables 6.1 and 6.2). Illustrations can include diagrams, tables, or models of your phenomenon. Photographs or links to videos can be used as well, which can be especially helpful for arts-based qualitative methods.

The following paragraphs provide a few strong quotes from the sample articles. The following quote brings to life the experience of an administrator in a workplace when dealing with a consumer:

> He would get really upset when he had to talk to people, he would get really nervous, he could go hide. He had the ability, but . . . a lot of times he would call me and just be in a panic and like, "Oh my gosh, I think they're making fun of me," and you just had to talk to him and get him through that particular situation. (Phillips, Kaseroff, Fleming, & Huck, 2014, p. 392)

You can feel the urgency of the participant, and the close description of the interaction helps you imagine what this might feel like for the person who is speaking.

Although sometimes a longer quote can help readers comprehend the complexity or depth of feelings, a series of shorter quotes can be helpful as well. For instance, in a participatory action study of parents of children with emotional disability diagnoses, the following short quotes are highly evocative:

> The parents talked about their fatigue—it is "exhausting to be a father"—and despair—"I was crying all the time." They questioned whether they could continue to care for their children: "I can't do it. I can't be a parent." They felt helpless and overwhelmed because they did not know how to deal with their child's challenging behaviors and school failure. (Ditrano & Silverstein, 2006, p. 363)

The article continues to present similarly strong evidence for other stressors the parents faced.

▩ **Table 6.1.** Example of a Table to Display Findings and Their
Central Characteristics

Table X
Sexual Orientation Microaggressions in Psychotherapy

Theme	Microaggression	Message
Assumption that sexual orientation is the cause of all presenting issues	A therapist says to a client, "I know what the problem is, you are gay." When a client discusses academic issues, a therapist interjects, "What do you think this issue has to do with your sexuality?"	Your sexual orientation is the problem. Your sexual orientation needs to be treated.
Avoidance and minimizing of sexual orientation	A therapist avoids using LGBQ terminology. A therapist tells a client, "You don't have to worry about that [sexual orientation] right now, let's talk about this other issue." When a client is accidently outed, a therapist responds, "Good, it's about time."	Issues related to your sexual orientation are not important to talk about. You should feel uncomfortable talking about your sexual orientation. You make me uncomfortable. Coming out is not a big deal.
Attempts to over-identify with LGBQ clients	A therapist makes frequent references to distant family members who are LGBQ. A therapist tries to befriend LGBQ clients or frequently engages in small talk. A therapist changes the way he or she speaks or changes physical posture to appear more comfortable with LGBQ individuals.	I understand your issues because I know someone who is LGBQ. I am not homophobic because I know someone who is LGBQ. You are an oddity, and I am "cool" because I work with you.

Table 6.1. (*Continued*)

Table X
Sexual Orientation Microaggressions in Psychotherapy

Theme	Microaggression	Message
Making stereotypical assumptions about LGBQ clients	A gay male client describes his weekend and the therapist says, "You were in a hardware store?!" A therapist tells an attractive lesbian woman, "You don't look like a lesbian."	All LGBQ people are alike. I don't need to make an effort to get to know you as an individual.
Expressions of heteronormative bias	An LGBQ client notices that a therapist's office only displays heterosexual books and pamphlets. After a client discloses their sexual orientation, a therapist states, "I am not gay!"	You are abnormal. You need to change or conform.
Assumption that LGBQ individuals need psychotherapeutic treatment	A therapist encourages a client to stay in treatment against the client's wishes. When a client is being referred, the referring therapist states, "It doesn't matter who you see as long as you're seeing someone."	LGBQ identities are pathological and need treatment. You are inherently flawed.
Warnings about the dangers of identifying as LGBQ	A therapist asks a client, "Are you sure you want to enter this lifestyle?" or "Have you really thought this through?" When a client discusses experiencing discrimination, the therapist says, "This lifestyle brings certain problems with it."	You are incapable of making rational decisions. Any problems you face are your own fault for choosing an LGBQ identity. Systemic oppression does not exist.

Note. LGBQ = lesbian, gay, bisexual, and queer. From "Sexual Orientation Microaggressions: The Experience of Lesbian, Gay, Bisexual, and Queer Clients in Psychotherapy," by K. Shelton and E. A. Delgado-Romero, 2011, *Journal of Counseling Psychology, 58*, p. 215. Copyright 2011 by the American Psychological Association.

Table 6.2. Example of a Table to Display Hierarchical Findings

Table X
*Cluster, Category Subcategory Titles, and the Numbers of Studies
that Contributed Meaning Units to Each*

Clusters	Categories
Cluster 1. Therapy Is a Process of Change Through Structuring Curiosity and Deep Engagement in Pattern Identification and Narrative Reconstruction (71)	Category 1.1: Curiosity drives reflexivity, transference, and relationship pattern analysis leading to new interpersonal strategies. (25) Category 1.2: Fear of sadness and vulnerability prompts disengagement but experiencing and exploring these emotions in therapy enhances engagement and leads to acceptance. (36) Category 1.3: The structure and support from the therapist helps clients to identify and change behavior patterns in their lives. (29) Category 1.4: The analysis of thoughts and assumptions can lead to the generation of new options and possibilities. (20) Category 1.5: Reflexivity leads to holistic awareness and a new self-narrative, abetted by therapists' insights. (48)
Cluster 2. Caring, Understanding, and Accepting Therapists Allow Clients to Internalize Positive Messages and Enter the Change Process of Developing Self-Awareness (82)	Category 2.1: Authentic caring lets clients feel validated and engage in vulnerable discussion, however, overinvolvement can limit their sense of agency. (61) Category 2.2: Being deeply understood and accepted helps clients engage in self-reflection nondefensively and increase their self-awareness. (56) Category 2.3: Internalizing the accepting therapist allows client change inside therapy and creates positive changes to external relationships. (18) Category 2.4: Feeling unheard, misunderstood, or unappreciated challenges the alliance and requires discussions of differences. (25)
Cluster 3. Professional Structure Creates Credibility and Clarity but Casts Suspicion on Care in the Therapeutic Relationship (54)	Category 3.1: The therapist's professional status aids in credibility. (33) Category 3.2: Professional context creates clarity but can undermine the authenticity of the relationship, make therapy inaccessible, or foster dependence. (36)

■ **Table 6.2.** (*Continued*)

Table X
*Cluster, Category Subcategory Titles, and the Numbers of Studies
that Contributed Meaning Units to Each*

Clusters	Categories
Cluster 4. Therapy Progresses as a Collaborative Effort With Discussion of Differences (59)	Category 4.1: Explicitly negotiating client–therapist roles when setting the therapy agenda lessens the clients' sense of a problematic power imbalance. (38) Category 4.2: Cross-cultural differences can be managed by exploring differences and valuing the individual within the culture. (31)
Cluster 5. Recognition of the Client's Agency Allows for Responsive Interventions That Fit the Client's Needs (72)	Category 5.1: Clients are agents of both engagement and disengagement. (62) Category 5.2: Clients wish therapists to be responsive by checking on their goals, the fit of the process, and the content of sessions, but to provide guidance when blocked or when avoiding key issues. (46)
Core Category: Being Known and Cared for Supports Clients' Ability to Agentically Recognize Obstructive Experiential Patterns and Address Unmet Vulnerable Needs (109)	

Note. From "A Qualitative Meta-Analysis Examining Clients' Experiences of Psychotherapy: A New Agenda," by H. M. Levitt, A. Pomerville, and F. I. Surace, 2016, *Psychological Bulletin, 142,* p. 817. Copyright 2016 by the American Psychological Association.

Quotes show how a finding was observed or interpreted from data and increase readers' confidence in the finding. For instance, in the study on Black heterosexual men's masculinity and safe sex (Bowleg, Heckert, Brown, & Massie, 2015), the following excerpt from the focus group dialogue provides a foundation for the finding "The Condom as 'Safe' Woman Signifier Construction," which might be hard to understand in its absence:

Focus group facilitator: So, women don't—so, in your experience women don't necessarily bring that conversation up [using condoms]. . . . But do women talk to you guys about [condoms]?

Speaker 1: . . . You have any condoms, so I ain't got to use mine. I [don't have] [laughter] mine in my wallet [because] the last time I used it [a condom].

Speaker 2: That's dangerous there . . . usin' their [a woman's] condom.

Speaker 1: No. I use mine. I use mine. No, that's why there ain't nothing [no condom] in there. Now, when I go home, I gotta put another one in [my wallet].

Focus group facilitator:	Wait. So wait. So hold up. So, why do you say that though? About using a woman's condom be dangerous? 'Cause it's (.) they might put a hole in it? So you think it might be a set-up?
Speaker 3:	Entrapment!
Speaker 2:	I had a woman tell me she was allergic to condoms. Do you know how fast I took off the other way? (p. 318)

It is clear from the quote the multiple ways participants thought condoms provided safety in the face of an attitude of suspicion in female sexual partners.

The text surrounding the quote can situate the quote and help its meaning come clear. In the following excerpt from an article on the academic trajectories of immigrant youth (Suárez-Orozco et al., 2010), a case study summary is presented with quotes peppered through it:

> Ironically, considering the brutality that Marieli witnessed in Guatemala, she finds that one of the worst things about her new land is the violence: "In Guatemala, there was less danger, more freedom." Marieli's neighborhood is a hub of gang activity. She laments being *encerrada* (locked in): "You can't go anywhere or leave your house because something might happen to you," she complains. Her negative perceptions of America increase over time as she witnesses and experiences discrimination aimed at people who lack residency papers and cannot speak English. She also reports high levels of ethnic tension and violence at school: "A lot of things can happen to you in school," she says. "A group of kids can still beat you down. There are only five security guards, and they can't cover the whole school. Last week, there was a fight, and a female teacher stepped in to separate them, and they hit her. Cut her face. Lots of blood." (p. 611)

The text around the quotes helps readers see Marieli's situation and makes vivid the struggles she is facing. Across all of these examples, you can see how the quotes help readers obtain a strong sense of the individuals' experiences and appreciate the emotions, social dynamics, and thoughts that might be related to a phenomenon.

Quantifying Results

Findings may or may not include quantified information, depending on the study's goals, approach to inquiry, and study characteristics. Some traditions of qualitative research routinely quantify their findings, and others do not (see also Maxwell, 2010). Many methods answer questions of what or how (e.g., What are the social practices at play here? How do people experience a phenomenon? How does power function in this system? What is the meaning of this phenomenon for people?). Quantification may not add to the answers to these questions. Other research goals, however, can benefit from quantification. For instance, researchers working to mask the taste of a drug might wish to report the proportion of participants in their focus groups who said they liked chocolate when asked. Quantifying results in this way can be useful as it can help increase the utility of the findings of a research study. Some studies use a mixed methods approach that blends qualitative and quantitative methods, which I discuss in more detail in Chapter 9. It is important, however, to use quantification in ways that have integrity within the research design.

For instance, if your study uses semistructured or unstructured interviews, it may not make sense to report the numbers of participants who indicated a certain response. These forms of interview may have one or a few central questions but may be adapted to participants' interests and focus, allowing for depth of inquiry into the areas of most concern for each participant. If all participants are not asked the same question point-blank (e.g., "Do you like the smell of chocolate?"), however, some participants might have indicated agreement to that question but did not comment on that aspect because they were focused on other aspects (e.g., the taste of chocolate, its appearance, its cost, their preference for fruit filling). Quantifying results and presenting them as though they indicate the proportion of agreement, then, can be misleading.

Instead, researchers who are interested in quantification might report on these findings as indicating the salience of an issue for participants, which might or might not be meaningful depending on the research question. Or researchers can ask participants the same question point-blank if they are seeking feedback and then report the extent of agreement across their responses. In any case, if you decide to quantify your results, you want to provide some guidance to your readers on how to interpret those numbers (e.g., as indications of salience or agreement). Also, a recent metamethod study found that most qualitative researchers do not quantify their findings (Levitt, Pomerville, Surace, & Grabowski, 2017), so this practice was not found to be routinely expected.

Developing Findings That Answer Your Question

In my experience as an associate editor and reviewer, probably the most common reporting problem I see is the tendency for researchers to produce findings that replicate their questions. For instance, if your question is, "What is the experience of being an activist?" you may have questions like the following: "How did you become an activist?" "What actions are entailed in your activism?" and "What are the challenges related to being an activist?" If your core findings (e.g., themes, categories, descriptions) then are "Becoming an Activist," "Actions Entailed in Activism," and "Challenges Related to Activism," then the categories you have developed are all restatements of the questions you asked, rather than answers to those questions. There is little point in having conducted a study only to find out your questions. Better findings might be "People Become Activists After Witnessing Battles Against Injustice," "Defining Actions in Activism Include Educating Others and Modeling Resistance to Oppression," and "Challenges Center Around Being the Target of Prejudice by Those Both Near and Distant." A study that finds answers that replicate your questions (which you knew at the outset!) does not have either fidelity or utility. As a result, it is better to have your findings (e.g., category or theme titles) worded so that they capture the answers to your questions. Often when I review these studies, I can see that there are answers inherent in the data presented, and sometimes the answers are alluded to in the descriptions of the findings, but the researchers failed to formulate them. As described before, this method of reporting leaves it up to readers to make sense of the findings and draw conclusions. Instead, it is the work of the researchers to conduct and present the analysis lucidly so the understanding they have gained becomes accessible to readers. The *Publication Manual of the American Psychological Association* also notes the importance of reporting results that don't match your expectations, including "uncomfortable results" you might be tempted to hide by omitting them (6th ed.; American Psychological Association, 2010, p. 32).

Considerations Regarding Results Section Length

The need to present material to exemplify your work is the reason why qualitative Results sections tend to be longer than quantitative Results sections. Selecting material carefully can help in this process, but lengthy manuscripts are almost unavoidable because the assessment of aspects of methodological integrity (groundedness, contextualization, and coherence) depends on detailed description. In addition to permitting the space needed for qualitative manuscripts, journals may develop guidance for authors to place supplemental materials online. This space can benefit the field by allowing the methodological integrity of qualitative research to be more comprehensively evaluated.

What Does It All Mean? The Discussion Section

The Discussion section is the place in which you position your paper to have an impact on the field. Now readers know what you have found, but they haven't considered yet how important those findings are or how they can be of use. Although you may have been deeply engaged in your research and it might seem evident to you how revolutionary your ideas are or how they might contribute to the literature, your readers have not had this lived experience. You want to return to the initial framing of your research story and revisit the debates and concerns you laid out in the introduction. Your readers will be interested in your explanation of how your research contributes to your field of study in light of the concerns you raised before. You want to tie up loose ends so the ramifications of your findings are clear.

In addition, the Discussion section is the moment in the story when you can make clear to readers how they can appropriately make use of your findings and also caution them about the limitations of your work. It can be important to consider the people who compose your readership when writing this section. You might have guidance for researchers on how to design studies to answer gaps in your findings or how to deepen the understanding you have contributed. You might make suggestions for practitioners on how to use your findings to advance health care, improve education, or provide treatments. Depending on the nature of your findings, you might incite readers to make changes in their own behaviors or to foster positive social changes. In addition to practical contributions, your work might advance theory and conceptualization in an area of psychology and lead to a new vision of your subject matter. In any case, your recommendations will need to be clear in order to contribute to your field and make it more likely that your article will make a difference.

http://dx.doi.org/10.1037/0000121-007
Reporting Qualitative Research in Psychology: How to Meet APA Style Journal Article Reporting Standards, by H. M. Levitt

In some qualitative traditions, the Results and Discussion sections are presented in an intertwined manner under the heading Findings (e.g., Bamberg & Georgakopoulou, 2008), with perhaps a brief conclusion at the end. Although this format is less common in psychology, this form of presentation may be more congruent for research traditions in which the results are conceptualized as coconstructed or interpretive as it does not suggest that the results are absent of interpretation in contrast to the discussion. In addition, there can be less redundancy if the implications of findings are discussed as they are presented.

Orientation Paragraph of Central Findings' Implications

At the beginning of your Discussion section,

■ describe the central contributions and their significance in advancing disciplinary understandings.

You may include some reflection on how your own perspective has changed in the process of gaining these understandings.

Often a Discussion section begins with a paragraph that summarizes the central finding of a paper and orients readers to the main implications that will be considered within that section. Typically, the paragraph does not restate all your results but focuses on transitioning from the last paragraph in your Results section that summarized and organized your findings into a focus on their implications for the field. Usually this paragraph is brief but shifts readers to thinking about the findings in relation to their impact. For instance, the following paragraph in a task analysis of emotional processing highlights the main finding of that study (Pascual-Leone & Greenberg, 2007):

> Prior to this investigation, the most thorough emotion-based model of how clients' experiences of bad feelings actually change in therapy was that of Greenberg and Paivio (1997). Consequently, many of the steps in that model served as null hypotheses for the discovery phase regarding components for processing emotional distress. The new model both confirms this model and develops an original model of how bad feelings are restructured through emotional processing. Overall, progression through the model describes a differentiation of emotion states from global to more specific feelings/meanings. . . . This supports work by Stern (1997), who argued within contemporary psychoanalytic theory that working through distress begins by helping clients interpret raw, unformulated, "global" experiences. (Pascual-Leone & Greenberg, 2007, p. 884)

You can see how this opening highlights the main contribution of the findings in that study and then continues by considering the various implications of the new model.

Reflexive Reflections

Through your research narrative or in a separate subsection, you might describe whether your perspective changed over the course of your study. You might find that you began the study with a belief on your topic that was challenged, forcing you to rethink your position, your values, or your own identities. Readers will be interested in hearing how your position shifted as this contextualizes your findings. Often I find that reviewers are interested in hearing what was surprising in a study or, depending on your approach to inquiry, how findings in a study were used by the participants or the research team. This self-reflective text might be described within one subsection or might run throughout the discussion of your results.

Contributions of Your Research

In your Discussion section,

- describe the types of contributions made by findings (e.g., challenging, elaborating on, and supporting prior research or theory in the literature describing the relevance) and how findings can be best utilized,
- identify similarities and differences from prior theories and research findings, and
- reflect on any alternative explanations of the findings.

There are a number of ways that your research might contribute to your field. There are many ways in which research can contribute to solving a problem. These will depend in part on the nature of your research question and the epistemological approach to your study. Your study could have generated future research directions, clinical guidance, theoretical advances or challenges, pragmatic solutions, deepened understandings, consciousness raising, social action suggestions, or strengthened support for past research, among many other forms of contributions. Considering the varied ways in which your work might be valuable can allow you to create an outline to guide you in writing the subsections of your Discussion section.

Remembering that you can describe your contribution in any of these ways (and I'm sure others as well!) can help you consider how to style your research narrative. It can be easy for authors to fall back on a style in which they point only to the deficits of prior research in order to bolster their own work. This is a narrative trope that has a long history and may resonate with some readers. There are dangers to this approach, however. Some papers exaggerate flaws in prior research either that were unavoidable or that are recreated in their own work. For instance, a critique of research on retrospective accounts without any recognition of the advantages of that form of data collection will not be as well received as a more balanced account. Or a study harshly critiquing earlier work for not having made use of recent advances or insights that were unavailable at the time may seem inappropriate. (Also, this approach may not make friends of your colleagues who have conducted this work—and who may end up reviewing your paper.) Instead of tearing down prior research, an approach I prefer is to give credit to past authors for their foundational contributions and then show how my work builds from theirs. Identifying similarities to and differences from prior theories and research findings can allow readers to see how your work is grounded in established understandings while they note what it offers.

Another problem to avoid is oversimplifying prior research instead of presenting findings in appropriate complexity. Describing the types of methods used in prior research, the perspectives held by prior investigators, and the context at that time or location allows you not only to be accurate in your reporting but also to engage in a deeper conversation with that work. Generally, the closer the research is to your own work, the more detailed its description should be so that readers understand where your work and the other work depart and why that might be.

It is helpful to describe the implications that your research holds, which might fall across multiple spheres. Your work might shed light on theories, provide new directions for future research activities, suggest educational or health care strategies, or contribute in other ways. As you describe the implications of your work, you want to refer to the literature that suggests that the directions you recommend might be profitable to pursue. Remembering to bolster the description of each contribution with references to past work will strengthen your work's perceived utility and encourage readers to see the value in your suggestions.

As you consider the implications of your research, you want to reflect on not only the literature that supports your ideas but also alternative explanations of findings. Consider the contexts of the other research with which your work is in conversation and how they relate to your own study. It will be particularly important to situate your contributions in light of prior qualitative research, as these methods might be expected to find more similar forms of results to your own. Did you adopt a different perspective on your question than prior researchers or come to the study from a different background or set of assumptions? Did you have a different data source or use a different method of analysis? You can consider how your social and professional situations might bear influence on your findings in comparison with that of prior researchers.

You can take this opportunity to rebut ideas that are inconsistent with your work or argue why your explanations are stronger. It also might be that your explanations make a contribution even if they are not stronger because they complement or clarify prior research. Instead, you might use the Discussion section to differentiate when your findings might apply and when prior research still holds. You might consider whether there are differences between your contexts or populations or the dynamics at play that might be contributing toward conflicting findings in the research. Also, you can identify future research strategies to explore these conflicts more extensively.

Limitations and Strengths

In your Discussion section

- identify the study's strengths and limitations (e.g., consider how the quality, source, or types of the data or the analytic processes might support or weaken its methodological integrity);
- describe the limits of the scope of transferability (e.g., what should readers bear in mind when using findings across contexts);
- revisit any ethical dilemmas or challenges that were encountered, and provide related suggestions for future researchers; and
- consider the implications for future research, policy, or practice.

In your Discussion section, it is expected that you consider the implications of your findings to assist your readers in understanding their potential use. These implications can extend across many areas, including training, practice, education, policy, and future research. Whenever possible, it is advantageous to describe how your work advances multiple spheres—for instance, moving forward both future empirical research and theoretical conceptualization.

As you discuss the use of your results, you will be expected to consider how your method might have limited the transferability of your findings or of the theoretical contributions you have made. *Transferability* is the ability of readers to take the findings you have presented and apply them to their own contexts, population, or settings. As a researcher, you want to aid them in this process by indicating the context of your own study clearly and by indicating how you think findings may or may not transfer.

For instance, if your study is on women who have been diagnosed with breast cancer, you might want to caution readers to use care when applying your results to women with other types of cancer, or to children with cancer, or to men or transgender people with cancer. You might consider, if the participants you interviewed were all in an urban area, how your findings might be different if the participants were located in a rural area and had to commute to receive health care. Or you might consider whether your participants had insurance or other means for paying for treatments and how your findings might differ if they did not. When considering issues that might affect transferability, you want to look in the literature to see what it suggests. Perhaps there is research that indicates that women in urban and rural areas have similar reactions except under certain conditions, which you then can clarify as important limiting factors. Or perhaps the research suggests that men with cancer have radically different reactions. In any case, providing this information will help your readers make decisions on how best to transfer your findings as they address their own questions.

Limitations

Typically in this process, you want to consider how the quality, source, or types of the data or the analytic processes might support or weaken your study's methodological integrity (see Chapter 3 for more guidance on how to establish methodological integrity). If there are shortcomings in your analysis, you want to be transparent about them to aid readers in assessing the findings. You might want to make recommendations for future research that encourage new investigators to avoid problems that you encountered. Also, if your findings have differences in rigor, you can point out how some findings were weaker and others stronger to guide readers' confidence in your work.

Sometimes authors remind readers that qualitative analyses can lead to multiple solutions. Investigators who hold alternative interests might develop findings that are equally rigorous, even if they focus on a similar topic. For instance, you might interview graduate students on their developing researcher identities with a keen interest in how they balance their other interests with this emerging identity. However, I might interview them with a keen interest in the role that curiosity plays and how curiosity is a privilege that might require development for many students. Although our findings might both hold integrity, we might not expect that our findings will replicate one another. Many qualitative approaches hold that there may be more than one valid and useful set of findings from a given data set.

Presenting the limitations of your study acts to increase readers' confidence in your study as it portrays your analysis as having been conducted with caution and concern not to overstate your findings. A nice example can be found in Frost's (2011) study of how stigma influences couples' intimacy in same-sex relationships:

> The results of this study should be interpreted in light of several limitations. Only individuals currently in relationships of two or more years were eligible for the study. The experiences of formerly partnered and newly partnered individuals are important to take into consideration given the relationship between stigma and intimacy may be experienced differently across relationship stages (e.g., formation, dissolution). Data were further limited to one partner's perspective. Dyadic data may provide additional insight into the processes under investigation in the current study. Further, the frequencies with which strategies were used in participants' narratives are not generalizable, and were reported here for the sole purpose of describing the data.
>
> Additionally, experiences of stigma in populations of low socioeconomic status and racial/ethnic minorities may not be well-represented in the sample. The analytical focus was limited to sexual orientation stigma, and was not sensitive to the intersectional experience of multiple forms of marginalization (i.e., interracial same-sex couples). Given these populations often experience the highest levels of minority stress (Meyer et al., 2008), experiences of stigma may have been underrepresented in the current study. (p. 8)

You will see by looking at the quote in the following section how the considerable strengths of Frost's study remain even after these limitations are acknowledged.

As illustrated in the example above, this part of your manuscript allows you to make suggestions for how to improve research in the future. Especially in cases where ethical issues arose in the process of conducting the study, it will be important to advise future researchers how to anticipate and avoid those issues.

Strengths

It is important to make clear the limitations of your research, but your Discussion also provides you an opportunity to describe its strengths in terms of both unique findings and methodological rigor. It can remind readers that although your study has limitations, as all research does, there is still value in the work you have conducted. For instance, you might remind readers that research on the question you are exploring is lacking and why it is needed (just being rare is not sufficient reason to conduct research!) and briefly review the procedures you used to increase your study's methodological integrity.

A sample paragraph from Frost's (2011) article follows his paragraph on limitations (presented in the preceding section):

> Despite these limitations, the current study's use of a narrative approach represents a novel and meaningful contribution to the study of stigma and its impact on same-sex couples. Utilizing relationship stories as the primary unit of analysis produced an understanding of stigma that both complements and complicates previous research on stigma, minority stress, and same-sex couples. Thus, the findings portray a nuanced understanding of how couples experience stigma

in their everyday lives. A narrative approach may be useful in studies of other marginalized relationships (e.g., interracial, age-gap), as well as within studies of stigma outside of the context of relationships. Furthermore, the kind of idiographic and person-centered perspectives that relationship stories afford may be useful in informing clinical and counseling interventions designed to improve the lives of couples struggling with stigma and intimacy. (pp. 8–9)

These highlights assist the reader to value the features of your design that strengthen your methodological integrity.

Concluding Paragraph

The final paragraph (or two) at the end of a paper contains the information you most want the reader to recall. Often it is a provocative summary of the main findings, a call to action, a plea for future inquiry, or a statement of advocacy. After reading your paper, what do you want your readers to know, to do, to experience in a new way? The *Publication Manual of the American Psychological Association* states, "The concluding section may be brief or extensive provided that it is tightly reasoned, self-contained, and not overstated" (6th ed.; American Psychological Association, 2010, p. 36). Arczynski and Morrow (2017) ended their study with this brief yet powerful statement about feminist–multicultural supervision (FMS) of therapy practice:

> The future of FMS may bear supervisory contexts that empower clients, trainees, and supervisors to realize a vision of applied psychology that embodies respect for cultural difference and unflinchingly seeks to balance the scales of power in society at large. (p. 205)

The ending statements in a report can be powerful because they can now draw on all the work that has come earlier in your paper that has laid out carefully your perspectives and grounded them in your empirical research. I encourage students to take time with this paragraph so it can have an impact. After all the work you have done, you want your paper to be one that your readers remember!

Reporting a Qualitative Meta-Analysis: Key Features

O ften topics that are important in a given field are investigated by many sets of researchers. Research reports may describe investigations using a variety of methods. Pressing questions may be studied using multiple perspectives and groups of participants. Once a number of studies have been conducted on one topic, it can be beneficial to examine them together. Such an aggregate analysis can allow the research community to identify strong trends that endure across studies, to examine the ways researchers' perspectives influenced their findings, and to identify findings that should be questioned. This is the purpose of meta-analysis.

If you are interested in reading about the state of findings in a literature or an interpretation of that literature, a meta-analysis is the kind of article you would search for. If you are interested in contributing your interpretation of a field of research, this is the kind of study you might wish to conduct. When analyzing qualitative articles, these reviews most often are called *qualitative meta-analysis* or *meta-synthesis* (e.g., Paterson, Thorne, Canam, & Jillings, 2001; Sandelowski & Barroso, 2007). In this chapter, I survey three forms of qualitative meta-analysis, then I review how to apply the Qualitative Meta-Analysis Article Reporting Standards (QMARS; Levitt, Bamberg, et al., 2018) to your own writing.

http://dx.doi.org/10.1037/0000121-008
Reporting Qualitative Research in Psychology: How to Meet APA Style Journal Article Reporting Standards,
by H. M. Levitt

Forms of Qualitative Meta-Analysis

There are a variety of types of meta-analysis, including

- *meta-analytic reviews:* integrative analyses of the findings of primary qualitative studies,
- *metamethod reviews:* examinations of the methods used in primary qualitative studies, and
- *critical* or *theory-driven reviews:* analyses of primary qualitative studies from the perspective of a specific theory.

There are a variety of qualitative meta-analytic methods that have been developed for different purposes and organized in varied ways (e.g., Paterson et al., 2001). In this chapter, I describe the main forms as meta-analytic reviews, metamethod reviews, and critical or theory-driven reviews. When setting out to conduct a review of qualitative studies, you want to consider the review method you select in relation to the goals you have for your research. The goals of review studies can be varied, including generating new understandings of findings, identifying new directions, questioning discourses in a field, and identifying methodological trends.

Meta-Analytic Reviews

Meta-analytic reviews are not only a narrative description of a body of research (sometimes called *narrative reviews*) but also an aggregation, reanalysis, and integration of findings. Qualitative meta-analytic researchers collect primary qualitative research studies along a single theme to examine patterns among them. In these studies, instead of collecting and analyzing data from participants, researchers collect and analyze the findings from primary studies.

Researchers might use a qualitative method based in one method to examine primary research that uses a variety of qualitative methods. For instance, *metaethnography* (Noblit & Hare, 1988) is a review of qualitative research using ethnographic strategies. The articles reviewed using that strategy may or may not include any primary ethnographic research (Wanat, Boulton, & Watson, 2016). Similarly, *meta–grounded theory methods* can use strategies from grounded theory to review research using a variety of methods.

Methods also can be combined in a qualitative meta-analysis to creatively meet a variety of goals. For instance, in a meta-analysis of the literature on clients' experiences in psychotherapy, I and my colleagues initially used a grounded theory method to develop a highly attuned hierarchy of categories that analyzed and organized the themes in 109 articles (Levitt, Pomerville, & Surace, 2016). After the hierarchy reached saturation, demonstrating that the analysis of further articles was not producing additional categories, they used a content analysis to sort findings from the remaining articles in the literature base into the established hierarchy. Using both these methods allowed the researchers to develop not only a grounded representation of the literature but also a description of a literature base too large to analyze using grounded theory.

Metamethod Reviews

Metamethod reviews are studies that focus specifically on the ways methods are applied and interpreted. They examine the epistemological soundness of a literature base to see whether methods are being applied in a manner that can lead to sound findings. They consider how applications of methods may have influenced the resulting findings, looking to see if an area of research has systematically misinterpreted a result or excluded a perspective. These reviews can identify trends in methods, procedures, epistemologies, values, and topics examined.

Metamethod studies also evaluate the limitations of methods, provide a historical review of methods, and document standardization of procedural norms in a field. For instance, in a study I conducted with collaborators, we found that authors tended to use procedures that are understood as typically objectivist (viewing research as more credible if judgments are agreed on by multiple sources), even when these procedures appeared to be discrepant with the framework they proposed for their analysis, which might view multiple perspectives as equally valid (Levitt, Pomerville, Surace, & Grabowski, 2017). We pointed to the need for greater consideration of authors' epistemological framework so researchers can describe how they adapted procedures to mesh with the authors' perspectives on their research.

Critical or Theory-Driven Reviews

Critical or *theory-driven* reviews examine a literature from a certain theoretical perspective. For instance, critical race theory might be used to examine the ways racial groups are misrepresented in a literature. Critical queer theory might be used to examine the ways heterosexism and scientific representations have been intertwined. Similarly, a critical interpretive metasynthesis is a method designed to study how vulnerable groups are studied and to identify issues related to representation, equality, and the effects of prejudices (e.g., Dixon-Woods et al., 2006). For instance, Farrelly and Lester (2014) examined 13 studies and found that the central obstacle for mental health users with psychosis in treatment was poor communication about the goal of treatment, leading to confusion about roles and conflicting needs and compromising the therapeutic relationship.

Critical or theory-driven reviews can examine both methods and findings. Whereas meta-analyses work to aggregate and synthesize findings and metamethod reviews examine trends in methods, critical reviews use theoretical lenses to identify gaps. The QMARS guidelines can assist in improving the reporting for diverse types of reviews. When reporting, you want to conduct your literature review and frame the Method, Results, and Discussion sections so they are appropriate given your goals.

Qualitative Meta-Analysis Article Reporting Standards

Most of the reporting standards for qualitative meta-analyses in the QMARS are similar to those for regular qualitative methods outlined in the Qualitative Journal Article Reporting Standards (JARS–Qual; Levitt, Bamberg, et al., 2018). Differences have to do in part with the translation from primary analysis to secondary analysis. This means that, typically, if you replace the description of methods in the JARS–Qual with a description of the review method you are using, the recommendations will stand. For instance, in the abstract it is recommended that authors report their meta-analytic strategies instead of primary methods. In the introduction, authors should describe how the problem being investigated had been approached in the literature, leading up to the need for a meta-analysis. In the sections that follow, I focus on the parts of a qualitative meta-analysis that are most distinctive from a primary qualitative study. Section 2.10 of the *Publication Manual of the American Psychological Association* (6th ed.; American Psychological Association, 2010), also notes that not all components of a meta-analytic report need to be included in the printed journal article. Some items can be presented as online supplemental materials, such as the list of citations of studies reviewed in the meta-analysis, as well as the table that describes these studies in more detail (see also my discussion of supplemental materials in Chapter 4).

Study Selection

In your description of data collection in a qualitative meta-analysis,

- provide a detailed description of how studies to be reviewed were selected, including search strategies and criteria for inclusion and exclusion, and rationale;
- describe search parameters (e.g., thematic, population, and/or method);
- identify the electronic databases searched, web searches, or other search processes (e.g., calls for papers); and
- indicate the final number of studies reviewed and how it was reached.

In the Method section, instead of focusing on participant selection and recruitment, as a meta-analyst you want to describe how you selected the studies you are researching. You should provide information on the databases or places you searched, search terms you used, and criteria for exclusion and inclusion. As in quantitative meta-analyses, you want to provide the final number of articles you reviewed and how you arrived at this number.

You want to provide the rationale for your approach to collecting primary studies as well. Although quantitative meta-analyses typically seek to review the entire body of research that addresses a question in order to calculate aggregated effect sizes, this may not be the goal of qualitative researchers. Qualitative meta-analysts may want to describe why and how they selected a set of studies in relation to their goal. Although some researchers might wish to identify central findings across a literature base and so may decide to comprehensively review all articles, others might have a goal to develop an overarching theory and may use an iterative sampling strategy in which they review articles until their theory obtains saturation. Critical researchers may seek to demonstrate how a discursive problem takes hold by analyzing articles in high-impact journals. Or researchers might use a theoretical sampling approach to seek out variations related to a population or topic of interest. They might deliberately seek a body of literature to review that contains maximum variation, or they might constrain variation in ways that are theoretically important. For example, when conducting a metamethod analysis, researchers may decide to select only articles that use a particular methodological approach. In any case, you want to develop a strategy for data collection that fits your research goals and to describe that strategy in relation to this rationale.

Minges et al.'s (2015) meta-analysis of the qualitative literature on youth screen time described that process in the following manner:

> The qualitative metasynthesis began with a systematic search of the literature to locate articles that used qualitative methodology to describe barriers and facilitators to sedentary behaviors among youth. Sources were identified by the first and last author through searches of the following electronic bibliographic databases with the assistance of a medical librarian: Ovid MEDLINE, Ovid EMBASE, Ovid PsycINFO, Scopus, and CINAHL between January 2001 and January 2014. Furthermore, use of contemporary screenbased technologies, such as tablets, handheld video games, and personal computers have only expanded in recent years, and these technologies were not widely available prior to the 2000s. Articles published from 2001 onward were selected because of the establishment of public health guidelines that recommend less than 2 hr of screen time per day (American Academy of Pediatrics, 2001).
>
> Keywords were selected for the database search focusing on the following fields: (a) behaviors, including such terms as sedentary, sedentary behavior, sedentary lifestyle, physical inactivity, or low energy expenditure; combined with (b) modes, including the terms computer, computer games, video games, TV (watching or viewing), screen time, screen-based entertainment, Internet, indoor, transportation, car, automobile, or bus; combined with (c) age and year limiters, and qualitative clinical queries and keywords. Conducting searches of primary qualitative studies can be a challenging process; therefore, qualitative search strategies were employed to capture the breadth of qualitative literature in each database. Search strategies encompassed oversight from a medical librarian, the use of database filters, and sensitivity and specificity algorithms to identify articles (McKibbon, Wilczynski, & Haynes, 2006; Walters, Wilczynski, Haynes, & Hedges Team, 2006; Wilczynski, Marks, & Haynes, 2007; Wong, Wilczynski, Haynes, & Hedges Team, 2004). (p. 383)

They went on to describe their exclusion and inclusion criteria and provide a flow diagram to illustrate their process (see Figure 8.1).

Studies Reviewed

When possible, in a qualitative meta-analysis describe the primary studies by providing the following information:

- year of publication,
- disciplinary affiliation of primary author,
- geographic location of the study,
- language of the study,
- method of data collection (e.g., interview, focus group, online),
- method of analysis (e.g., thematic analysis, narrative analysis, grounded theory),
- purpose of primary studies and differences (if any) from the main questions of the meta-analysis,
- number of participants, and
- recruitment method (e.g., snowball, convenience, purposive).

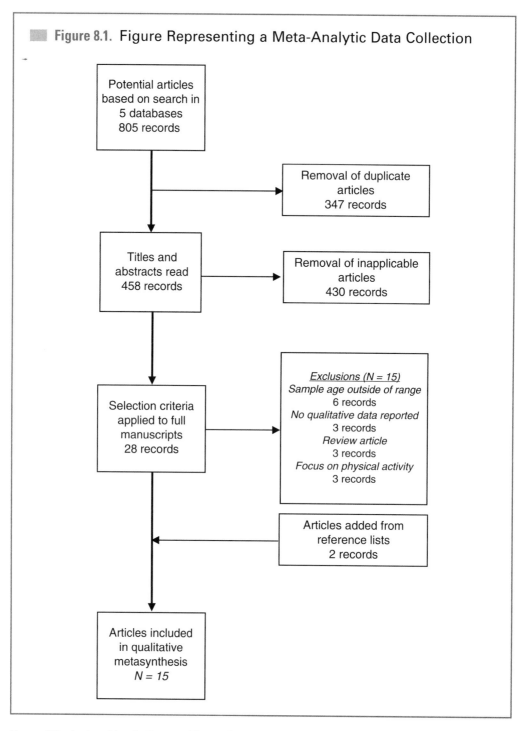

Figure 8.1. Figure Representing a Meta-Analytic Data Collection

Potential articles based on search in 5 databases 805 records

Removal of duplicate articles 347 records

Titles and abstracts read 458 records

Removal of inapplicable articles 430 records

Selection criteria applied to full manuscripts 28 records

Exclusions (N = 15)
Sample age outside of range
6 records
No qualitative data reported
3 records
Review article
3 records
Focus on physical activity
3 records

Articles added from reference lists 2 records

Articles included in qualitative metasynthesis *N = 15*

From "Reducing Youth Screen Time: Qualitative Metasynthesis of Findings on Barriers and Facilitators," by K. E. Minges, N. Owen, J. Salmon, A. Chao, D. W. Dunstan, and R. Whittemore, 2015, *Health Psychology, 34,* p. 389. Copyright 2015 by the American Psychological Association.

Instead of presenting information about your participants, in meta-analytic research you present information about the studies you have collected. This information typically includes the year of publication, methods of data collection and analysis used, questions asked, number of participants, and recruitment methods. This information often is presented in a table and summarized in the text.

Data Analysis

In your description of your data analysis in a qualitative meta-analysis,

- describe the approach to extracting study findings. This description may include the following:
  - description of coders or analysts and training, if not already described (interrater reliability, if used);
  - description of which parts of studies were assessed or appraised (e.g., abstract, Discussion, Conclusions, full article);
  - description of units for coding (words, concepts, interpretations);
  - description of software, if used;
  - description of team or collaborative discussions relevant to determining what constitutes findings of studies, how inconsistencies among analysts were managed, and how consensus was determined; and
  - discussion of whether coding categories emerged from the analyses or were developed a priori.
- describe the process of arriving at an analytic scheme, if applicable (e.g., if one was developed before or during the analysis or was emergent throughout);
- describe how issues of consistency were addressed with regard to the analytic processes (e.g., analysts may use demonstrations of analyses to support consistency, describe their development of a stable perspective, interrater reliability, consensus) or how inconsistencies were addressed;
- describe the appraisal process in cases in which some studies were considered to be more consequential in the interpretive process or others discounted; and
- describe how illustrations or other artistic products (if any) were developed from the analytic process.

When turning to describe your analysis, you want to describe how you extracted the main findings from the articles under review, in a manner similar to how you might describe your process of extracting findings from a set of interview responses or text in a primary study (see Chapter 3). Coders, methods of coding, parts of articles examined, research teams, and their processes all need to be described. Also, you want to report whether any coding was developed organically from the analysis of the text or whether the analytic scheme was developed prior to the analysis and then applied to the studies. As opposed to quantitative meta-analyses, weights to indicate the quality of primary research are not often applied to qualitative studies. This is because the vast majority of published studies can be expected to meet basic criteria for qualitative reviews. Also, these judgments would be challenging to create because differences in epistemological perspectives can make features that are strengths in one approach act as weaknesses in another (e.g., Levitt, Pomerville, et al., 2017).

For instance, if you are examining a study conducted by a team of investigators and use a process of consensus or interrater reliability, that process might demonstrate that multiple people support the interpretations made within that study. This would seem to improve the rigor of that study. If you are examining a study with one investigator who conducts all the interviews, codes and analyzes all the data, and has personal experiences with the phenomenon, that single investigator might understand the data more deeply than more casual investigators and might come to more profound understandings of the phenomenon under study. This would seem to improve the rigor of that study as well. As a result, it is difficult to compare qualitative methods or assign them ratings by simply checking off which procedures have been used. Using a perspective that examines methodological integrity holistically, in relation to the study goals, approach to inquiry, and study characteristics, is required (Levitt, Motulsky, Wertz, Morrow, & Ponterotto, 2017; see Chapter 3, this volume, on methodological integrity). This said, if any studies are discounted or if any are judged to be more consequential, it is important to describe the rationale for that decision and to be clear on that process.

Findings

When presenting the findings from a qualitative meta-analysis,

- describe the research findings and the meaning and understandings that the researcher has derived from the analysis of the studies;
- provide quotations from the primary studies to illustrate and ground the themes or codes identified, when relevant;
- explore whether differences in themes across primary studies appear to reflect differences in the phenomena under study or differences in the rhetoric or conceptual stances of the researchers;
- present findings in a manner that is coherent within the study design and goals (e.g., common themes, common interpretations, situated differences);
- consider the contexts of the meta-analytic findings as well as contradictions and ambiguities among the reviewed studies so that findings are presented in a coherent manner or discrepancies are addressed; and
- present synthesizing illustrations (e.g., diagrams, tables, models) if helpful in organizing and conveying findings.

When reporting findings of a qualitative meta-analysis, you want to present your analysis of the set of studies examined. Ideally, your findings will not only restate the findings of the primary literature but also shed new light on the set of studies examined. New theories, descriptions, and functions of a phenomenon may be articulated. Depending on the type of meta-analysis at hand, you may wish to examine the trends in the data in such a way that brings to light not only differences in findings, but also trends in rhetorical or conceptual positions of the researchers and the methods and research approaches used. This means that you want to examine the studies in context and help readers make sense of contradictions and ambiguities in the findings. Diagrams or tables can be helpful in presenting these findings coherently. Quotations or excerpts may be provided from the primary studies to illustrate this analysis.

You may wish to use quantification to present or summarize coding or study characteristics depending on the goals of your research. For instance, when analyzing trends in findings, discursive features, or methods, you might describe how frequently they occur. These numbers can act to support the qualitative analysis under way. It would be important, however, to be careful to interpret numbers appropriately, keeping in mind that all studies may not have asked the same questions, targeted similar participants or audiences, or used similar methods or approaches to inquiry (see the section in Chapter 6 on quantifying results). If the studies did not ask the exact same questions, the different frequencies of results cannot be interpreted as proportional to the total number of studies.

Describing the bases of claims being made can be helpful as well. For instance, if a set of findings is based on unusually strong empirical research, you want to describe why the findings are so well grounded. Or if they are based mostly on theoretical articles or case studies, you might add a note saying that the findings are more tentative or are based on certain types of cases or that more research is needed to strengthen confidence in those findings.

Situatedness

> To describe the perspectives of the researchers of the primary studies,
>
> - reflect on the situatedness of the studies reviewed (e.g., the positions and contexts of the primary researchers and their studies) and
> - simplify the complexity of displaying trends in studies by using tables as is helpful.

Situatedness is the only section that is entirely unique to qualitative meta-analyses and is not reflected in the JARS–Qual. It is typically considered within either the Results or Discussion section. *Situatedness* refers to the analysis of the positions of the primary researchers. (Because only meta-analyses are aggregating primary research studies, only they would consider the perspectives of the primary researchers of those studies.) Meta-analysts might consider the allegiance of the primary researchers to certain findings, their philosophical assumptions, their identities, their sociocultural context, the questions that motivated them, and their historical location (Zimmer, 2006). By examining tacit assumptions and contextual factors, researchers can bring to light the ways enclaves of researchers coalesce under certain mandates and how other perspectives might not be represented.

In Levitt, Pomerville, and Surace's (2016) meta-analysis on clients' experiences in psychotherapy, the Discussion section described how researchers investigating the effects of power looked at either cultural power (e.g., power related to class, race, sexual orientation, ability) or professional status (e.g., power related to being a professional), but not their interaction. The separation in these foci appeared to reflect the two different theoretical and research bases in which the primary researchers were situated:

> Research addressing the professional power of therapists has stemmed largely from humanistic researchers' work on how therapists inadvertently can block

clients' progress in therapy (e.g., Bohart, 2007; Rennie, 1994). In contrast, the multicultural researchers have focused upon issues related to cultural differences and oppression (e.g., Sue & Sue, 2012). The reconciliation of these two perspectives on power is recommended in future research to explore the ways that clients in therapy are influenced by interactions of these forms of power (Levitt, Whelton & Iwakabe, in press; Levitt, Whelton, Surace, & Grabowski, 2016; Comas-Diaz, 2012; Quinn, 2013). For instance, this work can shed light on findings related to ethnic differences in preferences for directiveness in therapy (e.g., LaRoche, 2002). (pp. 823–824)

Consideration of the traditions of researchers you are investigating and their allegiances can shed light on the types of findings they develop. This process can lead to recommendations for the field that shift the questions being asked or that raise awareness of their limitations.

Discussion

When discussing the findings of a qualitative meta-analysis,

- provide a discussion of findings that interpretively goes beyond a summary of the existing studies;
- include reflections on alternative explanations in relation to findings, as relevant;
- discuss the contributions that the meta-analysis makes to the literature (e.g., challenging, elaborating on, and supporting prior research or theory in the literature);
- draw links to existing scholarship or disputes in the literature that the meta-analysis is designed to address;
- describe the significance of the study and how findings can be best utilized;
- identify the strengths and limitations of the meta-study (e.g., consider how the quality or source or types of the data or analytic process might support or weaken its methodological integrity);
- describe the limits of the scope of transferability (e.g., what readers should bear in mind when using findings across contexts); and
- consider implications for future research, policy, or practice.

Many aspects of writing a Discussion section for a meta-analytic paper are similar to writing a Discussion section for a primary qualitative research paper. As when reflecting on results in a primary analysis, you want to describe what the meta-analysis has contributed to the literature. In a meta-analysis, you go beyond describing the findings of the studies to reach a new understanding of the literature as a whole. For instance, you might make clear whether there are emerging methods being used in the literature that offer a better description of the phenomenon, converging findings using differing terminology, new interpretations or understandings that appear superior, conflicting findings to be resolved, or associated methodological direction to the field. The implications of your findings can direct future researchers on how to best influence future clinical work, advocacy, policy, or education in relation to the trends you have observed.

You also want to describe the strengths and limitations of your research to make clear the quality of the studies you reviewed as well as the quality of your own study. Were there gaps in the primary literature that left unanswered questions? Were there issues related to the quality of analysis, types of data collected, or forms of analysis that restricted your confidence in your analysis? Did your analytic process focus on one area but leave other questions unanswered? Also, you should consider transferability in relation to the body of studies that have been examined and their characteristics. Make sure readers know what to keep in mind as they try to transfer the results of your study into their own contexts and populations.

Conclusion

As with primary analyses, meta-analyses can lead to multiple insights and understandings of the literature that each have methodological integrity. Although qualitative meta-analyses are relatively new methods, they provide a way to draw together prior qualitative research and lead to deeper understanding of the answers we are developing as a field and of the ways in which we ask questions.

Appendix 8.1:
Qualitative Meta-Analysis Article Reporting Standards (QMARS)

Table A8.1 Qualitative Meta-Analysis Article Reporting Standards (QMARS): Information Recommended for Inclusion in Manuscripts That Report Qualitative Meta-Analyses

Paper section or element	Description of information to be reported	Recommendations for authors to consider and notes for reviewers
Title page		
Title	Indicate the key issues/topic under consideration. Indicate that the work is a form of meta-analysis (e.g., qualitative metasynthesis, meta-ethnography, critical interpretive synthesis, review).	
Author note	Acknowledge funding sources or contributors. Acknowledge conflicts of interest.	
Abstract	State the problem/question/objectives under investigation. Indicate the study design, the types of literature reviewed, analytic strategy, main results/findings, and main implications/significance. Identify five keywords.	*Authors:* Consider using one keyword that describes the meta-analytic strategy and one that describes the problem addressed. *Authors:* Consider describing your approach to inquiry when it will facilitate the review process and intelligibility of your paper. If your work is not grounded in a specific approach to inquiry, or your approach would be too complicated to explain in the allotted word count, however, it would not be advisable to provide explication on this point in the abstract.

(table continues)

Table A8.1 (*Continued*)

Paper section or element	Description of information to be reported	Recommendations for authors to consider and notes for reviewers
Introduction		
Description of research problem/ question	State the problem/question the meta-analysis addresses.	
	Describe the importance or relevance of the meta-analysis to clarify barriers, knowledge gaps, or practical needs.	
Study objectives/research goals	Describe the meta-analytic method (e.g., metasynthesis, meta-analysis, meta-ethnography, thematic synthesis, narrative synthesis, or critical interpretive analysis).	
	Identify the purpose/goals of the study.	
	Describe the approach to inquiry, if it illuminates the objectives and meta-research rationale (e.g., descriptive, interpretive, feminist, psychoanalytic, postpositivist, critical, postmodern, constructivist, or pragmatic approaches).	
	Describe the contribution to be made.	
Method		
Research design overview	Summarize the research design, including data-collection strategies, data- or meta-analytic strategies, and, if illuminating, approaches to inquiry (e.g., descriptive, interpretive, feminist, psychoanalytic, postpositivist, critical, postmodern, constructivist, or pragmatic approaches).	*Reviewers:* This section may be combined into the same section as the objectives statement.
	Provide the rationale for the design selected.	

Study data sources

Researcher description	Describe the researchers' backgrounds in approaching the study, emphasizing their prior understandings of the phenomena under study (e.g., interviewers, analysts or research team). Describe how prior understandings of the phenomena were managed and/or influenced the research (e.g., enhancing, limiting, or structuring data collection and meta-analysis).	*Authors:* Prior understandings relevant to the meta-analysis could include, but are not limited to, descriptions of researchers' demographic–cultural characteristics, credentials, experience with phenomenon, training, values, and decisions in selecting archives or material to analyze. *Reviewers:* Researchers differ in the extensiveness of reflexive self-description in reports. It may not be possible for authors to estimate the depth of description desired by reviewers without guidance.
Study selection	Provide a detailed description of how studies to be reviewed were selected, including search strategies and criteria for inclusion and exclusion, and rationale. Describe search parameters (e.g., thematic, population, method). Identify the electronic databases searched, web searches, or other search processes (e.g., calls for papers). Indicate the final number of studies reviewed and how it was reached.	*Reviewers:* Qualitative meta-analyses may seek to review the literature comprehensively or may use iterative or purposive sampling strategies (e.g., maximum variation sampling, theoretical sampling, saturation seeking). In any case, the strategy should be described as well as the rationale for its use.

(table continues)

Table A8.1 (*Continued*)

Paper section or element	Description of information to be reported	Recommendations for authors to consider and notes for reviewers
Studies reviewed	Present, when possible, the following: • Year of publication of studies • Disciplinary affiliation of primary author • Geographic location of study • Language of study • Method of data collection (e.g., interview, focus group, online) • Method of analysis of study (e.g., thematic analysis, narrative analysis, grounded theory) • Purpose of primary studies and differences (if any) from the main questions of the meta-analysis • Number of participants • Recruitment method of study (snowball, convenience, purposive, etc.)	*Reviewers:* This information might be best presented in a tabular format, but it should also be summarized in the text.
Analysis		
Data-analytic strategies	Describe the approach to extracting study findings. This description may include the following: • Description of coders or analysts and training, if not already described (interrater reliability, if used) • Description of which parts of studies were assessed or appraised (e.g., abstract, Discussion, Conclusions, full article) • Description of units for coding (words, concepts, interpretations)	*Reviewers:* Findings of qualitative primary studies may be presented in disparate ways, and researchers should be transparent in making clear how they identified and extracted findings from primary reports. *Reviewers:* Typically, qualitative researchers do not assign numerical weights to findings in qualitative meta-analyses as the analyses are not statistical in nature.

(table continues)

- Description of software, if used
- Description of team or collaborative discussions relevant to determining what constitutes findings of studies, how inconsistencies among analysts were managed, and how consensus was determined
- Discussion of whether coding categories emerged from the analyses or were developed a priori

Describe the process of arriving at an analytic scheme, if applicable (e.g., if one was developed before or during the analysis or was emergent throughout).

Describe how issues of consistency were addressed with regard to the analytic processes (e.g., analysts may use demonstrations of analyses to support consistency, describe their development of a stable perspective, interrater reliability, consensus) or how inconsistencies were addressed.

Describe the appraisal process in cases in which some studies were considered to be more consequential in the interpretive process or others discounted.

Describe how illustrations or other artistic products (if any) were developed from the analytic process.

Methodological integrity   See the JARS–Qual standards.

Meta-analyses should describe the integrity of their secondary analyses as well as comment on the integrity of the primary studies under review.

Table A8.1 (*Continued*)

Paper section or element	Description of information to be reported	Recommendations for authors to consider and notes for reviewers
Findings/Results		
Findings/Results subsections	Describe the research findings and the meaning and understandings that the researcher has derived from the analysis of the studies.	*Reviewers:* Results sections tend to be longer than in quantitative meta-analyses because of the demonstrative rhetoric needed to permit the evaluation of the meta-analytic method.
	Provide quotations from the primary studies to illustrate and ground the themes or codes identified, when relevant.	*Reviewers:* Findings may or may not include the quantified presentation of relevant codes, depending on the study goals, approach to inquiry, and study characteristics.
	Explore whether differences in themes across primary studies appear to reflect differences in the phenomena under study or differences in the rhetoric or conceptual stances of the researchers.	
	Present findings in a manner that is coherent within the study design and goals (e.g., common themes, common interpretations, situated differences).	
	Consider the contexts of the meta-analytic findings as well as contradictions and ambiguities among the reviewed studies so that findings are presented in a coherent manner or discrepancies are addressed.	
	Present synthesizing illustrations (e.g., diagrams, tables, models) if helpful in organizing and conveying findings.	
Situatedness	Reflect on the situatedness of the studies reviewed (e.g., the positions and contexts of the primary researchers and their studies).	*Reviewers:* Situatedness can be considered in the Results or Discussion section.
	Simplify the complexity of displaying trends in studies by using tables as is helpful.	

Discussion

Discussion subsections		*Reviewers:* Rather than having only one possible set of findings, meta-analyses could lead to multiple insights and understandings of the literature that each have methodological integrity.
	Provide a discussion of findings that interpretively goes beyond a summary of the existing studies.	
	Include reflections on alternative explanations in relation to findings, as relevant.	
	Discuss the contributions that the meta-analysis presents to the literature (e.g., challenging, elaborating on, and supporting prior research or theory in the literature).	
	Draw links to existing scholarship or disputes in the literature that the meta-analysis is designed to address.	
	Describe the significance of the study and how findings can be best utilized.	
	Identify the strengths and limitations of the meta-study (e.g., consider how the quality or source or types of the data or analytic process might support or weaken its methodological integrity).	
	Describe the limits of the scope of transferability (e.g., what readers should bear in mind when using findings across contexts).	
	Consider implications for future research, policy, or practice.	

Note. Adapted from "Journal Article Reporting Standards for Qualitative Primary, Qualitative Meta-Analytic, and Mixed Methods Research in Psychology: The APA Publications and Communications Board Task Force Report," by H. M. Levitt, M. Bamberg, J. W. Creswell, D. M. Frost, R. Josselson, and C. Suárez-Orozco, 2018, *American Psychologist, 73,* pp. 38–40. Copyright 2018 by the American Psychological Association.

9

Reporting Mixed Methods Research: Bridging Reporting Standards

S o far in this book, we have discussed how to best report studies that use solely qualitative methods. This chapter describes the differences in reporting that occur when reporting *mixed methods*—that is, use of a qualitative and a quantitative method together in the same study. To continue the story-writing metaphor I've been weaving through this book, presenting a mixed methods article is not so much like telling two stories in an anthology; instead, it's like telling one story that contains two plot lines. To do this successfully, clearly position the central purpose of the story so that readers understand how the two plot lines are interconnected and how they enhance each other. If the two plot lines seem completely independent, there is no story. In this chapter, I review how the Mixed Methods Article Reporting Standards (MMARS; Levitt, Bamberg, et al., 2018) can help you merge the qualitative and quantitative aspects of your research to create a cohesive and engaging story for your readers.

In mixed methods studies, it is important to position the central question that holds together the qualitative and quantitative methods at the forefront of your work. This positioning allows you to show how both methods used build on each other to generate new insights. Studies should be designed intentionally so that the combination of the methods and the coanalysis will yield greater insight than if the studies were conducted independently (Creswell, 2013b; Greene, 2007; Tashakkori & Teddlie, 2010). The integration of qualitative and quantitative methods can lead to new understandings as the findings from each method shed light on each other. Although mixed methods studies sometimes result in separate manuscripts that portray qualitative and quantitative components, other times these components are presented together in one manuscript. This chapter focuses on the joint presentation style.

http://dx.doi.org/10.1037/0000121-009
Reporting Qualitative Research in Psychology: How to Meet APA Style Journal Article Reporting Standards, by H. M. Levitt

The field of mixed methods originated approximately 30 years ago, following a period of debates between qualitative and quantitative researchers. As a field it has grown rapidly, and now researchers across disciplines engage in this approach, and it boasts several dedicated journals (Onwuegbuzie, 2012; Small, 2011). Textbooks have articulated fundamental practices and described various mixed methods designs that can be useful in planning and communicating how qualitative and quantitative components can be integrated (e.g., Creswell, 2013b; Hesse-Biber, 2010). Although reporting standards have been developed by authors in the health sciences (e.g., Creswell, Klassen, Clark, & Smith, 2011) and by some journal editors (e.g., the *Journal of Mixed Methods Research*; Fetters & Freshwater, 2015), the MMARS guidelines developed by the Working Group on Journal Article Reporting Standards for Qualitative Research (Levitt, Bamberg, et al., 2018) are the first authoritative set of reporting standards that have been advanced in this context (see Table A9.1).

Although this chapter focuses on qualitative and quantitative analyses being reported together, some researchers combine two qualitative analyses in the same study. For example, in the article by Frost (2011), a content analysis and a narrative analysis were conducted together to achieve the researcher's aims. In those types of articles, the reporting of the analyses should follow the Journal Article Reporting Standards for Qualitative Research (JARS–Qual; Levitt, Bamberg, et al., 2018). Similar to the way that MMARS guides authors to discuss the goals and integrate the insights of qualitative and quantitative projects throughout their reporting, joining two qualitative analyses in one report should reflect the ways the two analyses enhance each other throughout the sections of the paper.

Most of the MMARS guidelines duplicate those for qualitative and quantitative research. When presenting qualitative components of a study, researchers generally should follow the JARS–Qual guidelines that have been described throughout this book (see Table A1.1). For the quantitative aspects, researchers should follow the Journal Article Reporting Standards for Quantitative Research (JARS–Quant; Appelbaum et al., 2018), which are listed in Table A9.2 (see also the *Publication Manual of the American Psychological Association*; 6th ed.; American Psychological Association, 2010; the JARS website at http://www.apastyle.org/jars/; Cooper, 2018). When components of a mixed methods study are presented together or in relation to one another, however, there are some important additions to be made. The rest of this chapter describes these additional components and their rationale.

Framing Your Mixed Methods Paper

When writing a mixed methods paper, you want to make clear from the start that both qualitative and quantitative methods are in use. Distinctive aspects of framing a mixed methods paper appear in the following sections:

- In the abstract,
  - indicate the mixed methods design, including types of participants or data sources, and analytic strategy, main results/findings, and major implications/ significance.

- In the objectives,
  - state three types of research objectives/aims/goals—qualitative, quantitative, and mixed methods—and order these goals to reflect the type of mixed methods design, and
  - describe the ways approaches to inquiry were combined, as it illuminates the objectives and mixed methods rationale (e.g., descriptive, interpretive, feminist, psychoanalytic, postpositivist, constructivist, critical, postmodern or constructivist, or pragmatic approaches).

Like Chapter 8 on qualitative meta-analyses, this chapter focuses on aspects that were not already discussed in the description of primary qualitative analyses but are particular to mixed methods papers. When considering a title for a mixed methods study, you want to select one that doesn't misrepresent your work as solely a quantitative or qualitative study. Using terms like *correlates* or *determinants* (how quantitative approaches sometimes conceptualize variables) or words like *phenomenological* or *experience* (how qualitative approaches sometimes conceptualize phenomena under study) can position a study within an epistemology that might not fit both parts of your research project. This means that you may want to focus your title on the issue at hand rather than a method. Or, if you would like to emphasize your methods, you might use the term *mixed methods* or reference both the qualitative and quantitative methods. Similarly, in the abstract, you want to describe the mixed methods design you used. Researchers are encouraged as well to use one of their keywords to indicate their mixed methods design. You can see the titles, abstracts, and keywords of two mixed methods papers (Meixner & O'Donoghue, 2013; Suárez-Orozco et al., 2010) in the appendix at the end of this book.

Throughout the paper (e.g., abstract, Method section, Results section), you want to deliberately make choices about the order in which you present the qualitative and quantitative components. The presentation should replicate the sequencing of these components as they were performed. When these components occurred together, you may use your discretion in presenting their sequencing. In making this decision, you can consider how to best present the narrative of your study and an audit trail that others who are interested in conducting similar work could follow (Merriam, 2014). Whatever choice you make, you want to consistently present your study components in that order throughout the paper.

In addition, you want to keep the mixed methods focus clear throughout the paper. In your objectives statement or at the beginning of your Method section, for instance, you want to describe not only the goals for the qualitative or quantitative components but also the goals for combining these approaches. For instance, Suárez-Orozco et al. (2010) described their goals for each component of their mixed methods study as follows:

> In the present study, we took a person-oriented perspective, which assumes that results are interpretable at the individual level (Magnusson, 1998), and used a complementary mixed-methods approach (Hammersley, 1996)—with each analytic approach providing a new level of insight (Bryman, 1996). We used latent growth modeling to describe trajectories of performance over time. We used multinomial logistic regression to delineate how indicators of family

characteristics, school characteristics, and individual characteristics were associated with academic trajectories. Moreover, we deepened our understanding
of academic trajectories of performance by implementing multiple case studies
(Yin, 2003).

   We used case studies to uncover unanticipated causal links, which quantitative data do not reveal, and to shed light on the developmental and interactional
processes at play (Yin, 2003). This mixed-methods approach allowed us to triangulate our findings and deepened our understanding of the challenges that
newcomer youth encounter as they enter U.S. schools. (pp. 604–605)

This framing continues through Suárez-Orozco et al.'s paper, and you want to continu-
ously frame your research in a similar manner throughout your report. What is the
rationale for having both a quantitative and a qualitative component? How are these
combined methods expected to enhance the understanding that can be gleaned from
each one? You want to answer these questions as you report your objectives and results
and discuss your findings.

Distinctive Features of Your Method

In the research design overview of a mixed methods paper,

- explain why mixed methods research is appropriate as a methodology given
  the paper's goals;
- identify the type of mixed methods design used and define it;
- indicate the qualitative approach to inquiry and the quantitative approach
  used within the mixed methods design type (e.g., ethnography, randomized
  experiment);
- if multiple approaches to inquiry were combined, describe how this was done
  and provide a rationale (e.g., descriptive, interpretive, feminist, psychoanalytic,
  postpositivist, critical, postmodern, constructivist, or pragmatic approaches),
  as it is illuminating for the mixed methods in use; and
- provide a rationale or justification for the need to collect both qualitative and
  quantitative data and the added value of integrating the results (findings) from
  the two databases.

   At the beginning of your Method section, you want to describe the mixed methods
design you used. Just as details about qualitative procedures are needed because they
are unfamiliar to many researchers, defining the term *mixed methods* is helpful. Also,
because *mixed methods* does not indicate a singular design, you need to describe the
specific type of design in use. There are a variety of names and types of mixed methods
designs that have been articulated. These typically describe the sequencing of the quantitative and qualitative components (e.g., Creswell, 2013b; Greene, 2007; Tashakkori
& Teddlie, 2010).

   Three basic mixed methods designs are the explanatory sequential design, the
exploratory sequential design, and the convergent design. An *explanatory sequential
design* begins with the quantitative component and then uses a qualitative component

to help interpret the quantitative findings. An *exploratory sequential design* begins with a qualitative component and then uses a quantitative component to further explore ideas initially developed or to evaluate those ideas, such as in a measure development project. A *convergent design* uses both qualitative and quantitative components concurrently in order to strengthen the understanding of the results of each component.

The introductory paragraph to the Method section in Meixner and O'Donoghue (2013) describes clearly the mixed method design they used, the purpose of the components of their research project, and the way the components were sequenced:

> This project entails a mixed methods design that is situated in an action research trajectory. Germane to most action research models is an underlying intent to change a system, challenge norms, and disrupt the status quo (Anderson & Herr, 2005; Argyris, Putnam, & Smith, 1985). Equally vital in action research is the empirical analysis of diverse perspectives, which can neither be ascertained by quantitative nor qualitative data alone. Mixed methods research entails collecting and analyzing statistical and narrative data to arrive at a more complex understanding of the research question (Creswell & Plano Clark, 2007).
>
> This study entailed two intersecting phases of data collection and analysis. The institutional review boards of a midsize public university and a state department of rehabilitative services approved both phases, respectively. Phase one involved the electronic distribution of a locally developed survey instrument. Comprising primarily quantitative questions, the survey also included embedded, open-ended response items. After a preliminary analysis of the phase one data, the research team designed and held 7 focus groups; questions were designed to explain quantitative findings and add depth to the analysts' understanding of the research phenomenon. Subsequent to the multirater coding of focus group data and a refined analysis of the survey data, the team concurrently interpreted data from both phases. Detailed information on participants, collection, and analysis is provided next. (p. 379)

This level of detail is helpful in orienting readers to the descriptions to come in the Method subsections and to how the components are interrelated.

In explaining your mixed methods in relation to the goals of your study, you want to present a convincing rationale for the design you used. An *implementation matrix* can be used to lay out in a tabular form the ways the aims of a study link to the strategies or processes used, the samples, the procedures, or the types of outcomes generated, if you find it to provide helpful orientation (Creswell et al., 2011).

In the description of participants or other data sources in a mixed methods paper,

- when data are collected from multiple sources, clearly identify the sources of qualitative and quantitative data (e.g., participants, text), their characteristics, as well as the relationship between the data sets if there is one (e.g., an embedded design); and
- state the data sources in the order of procedures used in the design type (e.g., qualitative sources first in an exploratory sequential design followed by quantitative sources), if a sequenced design is used in the mixed methods study.

In the sampling or selection, recruitment, and data analysis and quality descriptions in a mixed methods paper,

- describe the qualitative and quantitative sampling in separate sections;
- relate the order of the sections to the procedures used in the mixed methods design type;
- discuss the recruitment strategy for qualitative and quantitative research separately in mixed methods research;
- devote separate sections to the qualitative data analysis, the quantitative data analysis, and the mixed methods analysis; this mixed methods analysis consists of ways that the quantitative and qualitative results will be "mixed" or integrated according to the type of mixed methods design being used (e.g., merged in a convergent design, connected in explanatory sequential designs and in exploratory sequential designs); and
- indicate methodological integrity, quantitative validity and reliability, and mixed methods validity or legitimacy; further assessments of mixed methods integrity are also indicated to show the quality of the research process and the inferences drawn from the intersection of the quantitative and qualitative data.

Throughout the description of your methods, you want to make clear which component you are describing. For instance, is your participant recruitment summary describing the recruitment for only your qualitative or quantitative component, or for both? How about whatever sampling process you used? Presenting this information in two clearly demarcated sections can help readers disentangle the methods of your study. You want to make sure the order in which you conducted your procedures is clear.

A table often called a *diagram of procedures* (see Figure 9.1) can help you depict the sources of data collected for the qualitative and quantitative components and the procedures to which the data were subjected. This table can include information such as the format of data, when and from whom data were collected, and the types of questions or outcomes for the analysis of that data. Instead of describing data as "numeric" or "verbal," it is better to describe the type of data in reference to their purpose and goals. For instance, "nondirective interviews" or "Likert-scale ratings" better captures qualities of the data that can allow them to be analyzed effectively using different methods and philosophical approaches to analysis.

In the statements describing the researchers, mixed methods researchers may describe not only their background in qualitative research but also their expertise in both quantitative and mixed methods research. This information can help readers understand their background as they came to conduct the current research.

When describing data analyses, you should describe not only the qualitative and quantitative analyses clearly and separately but also the mixed methods analysis. The latter conveys how you integrated the two sets of results in order to benefit from having conducted both sets of analyses. Similarly, when describing the quality of your work, you want to describe not only the methodological integrity of your qualitative analyses and the validity of your quantitative analyses but also the basis for your process of integrating the two and for your conclusions. How did you use one set of findings to shed light on the other set? What did you do in order to ensure that the sets of findings were relevant to each other or that your interpretations were grounded in both sets of findings? Answers to these questions will strengthen readers' trust in your methods.

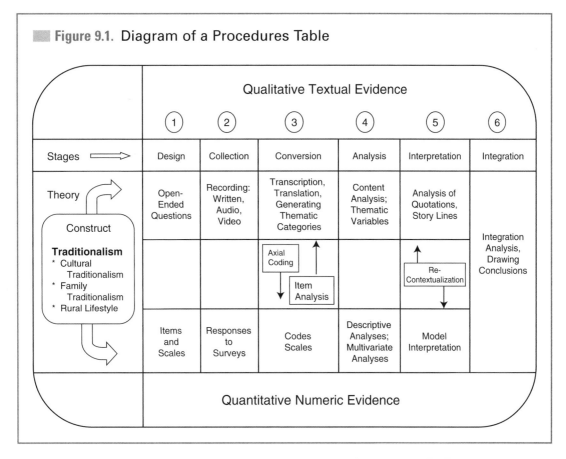

Figure 9.1. Diagram of a Procedures Table

From "Traditions and Alcohol Use: A Mixed-Methods Analysis," by F. G. Castro and K. Coe, 2007, *Cultural Diversity and Ethnic Minority Psychology, 13*, p. 271. Copyright 2007 by the American Psychological Association.

In the description of your analysis, you want to describe separately your qualitative and quantitative approaches. Using subheadings can help separate out these approaches. Similarly, when making a case for rigor of these components, validity, reliability, and methodological integrity should be described separately. For the sake of narrative flow, you may want these descriptions to follow the descriptions of the analysis of each component.

Distinctive Features of Your Results

When writing a mixed methods Results section,

■ indicate how the qualitative and quantitative results were "mixed" or integrated (e.g., discussion; tables of joint displays; graphs; data transformation in which one form of data is transformed to the other, such as qualitative text, codes, or themes transformed into quantitative counts or variables).

In the Results section, findings are usually separated into quantitative and qualitative components. These components should follow the same sequencing as in the other sections. Mixed methods researchers sometimes display their results using joint display tables or graphs that depict summaries of the qualitative and quantitative findings side by side (see Table 9.1). Researchers also can depict in a table or graph how the integration of both components leads to greater insight into the phenomenon by adding a column to show the integrated findings. This form of presentation allows researchers to directly compare and contrast the results from both components and to see the benefits from the mixed methods design. If data transformation is used to change one form of data into another (e.g., coding qualitative findings with numeric codes), the process of transformation should be made clear. Although Frost's (2011) study included two qualitative analyses and not a mixed methods analysis, it provides an example of transforming qualitative data into frequency counts of types of codes:

> The definitions used for coding intimacy were developed in a study of intimacy among gay men (Frost, Stirratt, & Ouellette, 2008). Each story was coded by

Table 9.1. Example of a Joint Display Table

Table X
Integrated Results Matrix

Quantitative results	Qualitative results	Exemplar quote
When the topic was *more* familiar (climate change) and cards were more relevant, participants placed *less* value on author expertise.	When an assertion was considered to be *more* familiar and considered to be general knowledge, participants perceived *less* need to rely on author expertise.	P144: "I feel that I know more about climate and there are several things on the climate cards that are obvious, and that if I sort of know it already, then the source is not so critical . . . whereas with nuclear energy, I don't know so much so then I'm maybe more interested in who says what."
When the topic was *less* familiar (nuclear power) and cards were more relevant, participants placed more value on authors with higher expertise.	When an assertion was considered to be *less* familiar and *not* general knowledge, participants perceived *more* need to rely on author expertise.	P3: "[Nuclear power], which I know much, much less about, I would back up my arguments more with what I trust from the professors."

Note. From "The Effects of Topic Familiarity, Author Expertise, and Content Relevance on Norwegian Students' Document Selection: A Mixed Methods Study," by M. T. McCrudden, T. Stenseth, I. Bråten, and H. I. Strømsø, 2016, *Journal of Educational Psychology, 108*, p. 157. Copyright 2016 by the American Psychological Association.

two independent raters: the author and an advanced undergraduate trained in qualitative methods. The resulting reliability coefficients (i.e., Cohen's kappa) for stigma- and intimacy-related content were .87 and .81, respectively. The content analysis identified 394 stories that contained intimacy-related themes and 166 stories that contained stigma-related themes. A total of 120 stories contained co-occurrences of stigma- and intimacy-related themes: 74 were in ambiguous story prompts, while 46 were in response to the stigma story prompt. Co-occurrences were distributed across 75 participants. (p. 4)

Frost also specified in the limitations section that these frequencies are not generalizable and that their purpose is to better describe the set of data under investigation.

Distinctive Features of Your Discussion

When writing a mixed methods Discussion section,

■ discuss the advantages and limitations of the mixed methods approach that you used.

Typically, the Discussion section, like the Method and Results sections, mirrors in sequence the procedures used in the type of mixed methods design. It also reflects on the implications of the integrated findings from across the two methods.

In the Discussion section, mixed methods researchers may describe the advantages of using the two approaches as well as the limitations. Although there may be implications that stem solely from the qualitative or quantitative analyses, researchers generally seek to discuss the implications of findings in a manner that reflects their integrated understanding. For instance, Meixner and O'Donoghue (2013) noted in their Discussion the following:

Of critical note, no hypotheses were formed given the nature of the mixed methods design and some may view this as a limitation. This design added rigor to the study—allowing the research team to expand, explore, and understand descriptive survey findings. That is, the strategic placement of the qualitative sequence allowed the research team to perform a preliminary analysis of the survey data, thus refining the qualitative (i.e., focus group) protocol. A systematic analysis of the qualitative data added a critical depth and perspective to a largely quantitative pool of literature. The mixing of quantitative and qualitative findings allows for the strengths of one method to offset the weaknesses of the other (Creswell & Plano Clark, 2007). (p. 384)

Comments like this that make clear how the sets of methods functioned to enhance one another in the study, as well as statements that integrate the specific findings, can be interspersed through the Results and Discussion sections. In the process of reporting mixed methods research, you want to make clear how both sets of methods deepened your understandings as well as the contributions that are being made to the literature.

Appendix 9.1:
Mixed Methods Article
Reporting Standards (MMARS)

Table A9.1. Mixed Methods Article Reporting Standards (MMARS): Information Recommended for Inclusion in Manuscripts That Report the Collection and Integration of Qualitative and Quantitative Data

Paper section or element	Description of information to be reported	Recommendations for authors to consider and notes for reviewers
Title page		
Title	See the JARS–Qual and JARS–Quant standards.	*Authors:* Refrain from using words that are either qualitative (e.g., *explore, understand*) or quantitative (e.g., *determinants, correlates*) because mixed methods stands in the middle between qualitative and quantitative research.
		Authors: Reference the terms *mixed methods or qualitative and quantitative*.
Author note	See the JARS–Qual and JARS–Quant standards.	
Abstract	See the JARS–Qual and JARS–Quant standards. Indicate the mixed methods design, including types of participants or data sources, and analytic strategy, main results/findings, and major implications/significance.	*Authors:* Specify the type of mixed methods design used. See the note on types of designs in the methods research design overview section below.
		Authors: Consider using one keyword that describes the type of mixed methods design and one that describes the problem addressed.
		Authors: Describe your approach(es) to inquiry and, if relevant, how intersecting approaches to inquiry are combined when this description will facilitate the review process and intelligibility of your paper. If your work is not grounded in a specific approach(es) to inquiry or your approach would be too complicated to explain in the allotted word count, however, it would not be advisable to provide explication on this point in the abstract.

(table continues)

Table A9.1. (*Continued*)

Paper section or element	Description of information to be reported	Recommendations for authors to consider and notes for reviewers
Introduction		
Description of research problems/questions	See the JARS–Qual and JARS–Quant standards.	*Authors:* This section may convey barriers in the literature that suggest a need for both qualitative and quantitative data. *Reviewers:* Theory or conceptual framework use in mixed methods varies depending on the specific mixed methods design or procedures used. Theory may be used inductively or deductively (or both) in mixed methods research.
Study objectives/aims/ research goals	See the JARS–Qual and JARS–Quant standards. State three types of research objectives/aims/ goals: qualitative, quantitative, and mixed methods. Order these goals to reflect the type of mixed methods design. Describe the ways approaches to inquiry were combined, as it illuminates the objectives and mixed methods rationale (e.g., descriptive, interpretive, feminist, psychoanalytic, post-positivist, constructivist, critical, postmodern or constructivist, or pragmatic approaches).	*Reviewers:* A mixed methods objective, aim, or goal may not be familiar to reviewers. It describes the results to be obtained from using the mixed methods design type where "mixing" or integration occurs (e.g., the aim is to explain quantitative survey results with qualitative interviews in an explanatory sequential design). For instance, the goal of a qualitative phase could be the development of a conceptual model, the goal of a quantitative phase might be hypothesis testing based upon that model, and the goal of the mixed methods could be to generate integrated support for a theory based upon quantitative and qualitative evidence.

Method

| Research design overview | See the JARS–Qual and JARS–Quant standards. Explain why mixed methods research is appropriate as a methodology given the paper's goals.

Identify the type of mixed methods design used and define it.

Indicate the qualitative approach to inquiry and the quantitative approach used within the mixed methods design type (e.g., ethnography, randomized experiment).

If multiple approaches to inquiry were combined, describe how this was done and provide a rationale (e.g., descriptive, interpretive, feminist, psychoanalytic, postpositivist, critical, postmodern, constructivist, or pragmatic approaches), as it is illuminating for the mixed method in use.

Provide a rationale or justification for the need to collect both qualitative and quantitative data and the added value of integrating the results (findings) from the two databases. | *Reviewers:* Because mixed methods research is a relatively new methodology, it is helpful to provide a definition of it from a major reference in the field.

Reviewers: Mixed methods research involves rigorous methods, both qualitative and quantitative. Refer to the JARS–Qual standards (qualitative) and JARS–Quant standards (quantitative) for details of rigor.

Reviewers: One of the most widely discussed topics in the mixed methods literature would be research designs. There is not a generic mixed methods design, but multiple types of designs. At the heart of designs would be basic, core designs, such as a convergent design, an explanatory sequential design, and an exploratory sequential design. Although the names and types of designs may differ among mixed methods writers, a common understanding is that procedures for conducting a mixed methods study may differ from one project to another. Further, these basic procedures can be expanded by linking mixed methods to other designs (e.g., intervention or experimental trial mixed methods study), to theories or standpoints (e.g., a feminist mixed methods study), or to other methodologies (e.g., a participatory action research mixed methods study). |

(table continues)

Table A9.1. (Continued)

Paper section or element	Description of information to be reported	Recommendations for authors to consider and notes for reviewers
Participants or other data sources	See the JARS–Qual and JARS–Quant standards. When data are collected from multiple sources, clearly identify the sources of qualitative and quantitative data (e.g., participants, text), their characteristics, as well as the relationship between the data sets if there is one (e.g., an embedded design). State the data sources in the order of procedures used in the design type (e.g., qualitative sources first in an exploratory sequential design followed by quantitative sources), if a sequenced design is used in the mixed methods study.	*Authors:* Because of multiple sources of data collected, separate descriptions of samples are needed when they differ. A table of qualitative sources and quantitative sources is helpful. This table could include type of data, when data were collected, and from whom. This table might also include study aims/research questions for each data source and anticipated outcomes of the study. In mixed methods research, this table is often called an *implementation matrix*. *Authors:* Rather than describe data as represented in numbers versus words, it is better to describe sources of data as open-ended information (e.g., qualitative interviews) and closed-ended information (e.g., quantitative instruments).
Researcher description	See the JARS–Qual standards.	*Reviewers:* It is helpful to establish in a publication the researchers' experiences (or research teams' experiences) with both qualitative and quantitative research as a prerequisite for conducting mixed methods research. *Authors:* Because mixed methods research includes qualitative research, and reflexivity is often included in qualitative research, we would recommend statements as to how the researchers' backgrounds influence the research.

Participant recruitment	
Participant sampling or selection	See the JARS–Qual and JARS–Quant standards. Describe the qualitative and the quantitative sampling in separate sections. Relate the order of the sections to the procedures used in the mixed methods design type.
Participant recruitment	See the JARS–Qual and JARS–Quant standards. Discuss the recruitment strategy for qualitative and quantitative research separately in mixed methods research.
Data collection	
Data collection/identification procedures	See the JARS–Qual and JARS–Quant standards.
Recording and transforming the data	See the JARS–Qual standards.

(table continues)

Table A9.1. (*Continued*)

Paper section or element	Description of information to be reported	Recommendations for authors to consider and notes for reviewers
Data analysis	See the JARS–Qual and JARS–Quant standards. Devote separate sections to the qualitative data analysis, the quantitative data analysis, and the mixed methods analysis. This mixed methods analysis consists of ways that the quantitative and qualitative results will be "mixed" or integrated according to the type of mixed methods design being used (e.g., merged in a convergent design, connected in explanatory sequential designs and in exploratory sequential designs).	
Validity, reliability, and methodological integrity	See the JARS–Qual and JARS–Quant standards. Indicate methodological integrity, quantitative validity and reliability, and mixed methods validity or legitimacy. Further assessments of mixed methods integrity are also indicated to show the quality of the research process and the inferences drawn from the intersection of the quantitative and qualitative data.	

Findings/Results

Findings/Results subsections

See the JARS–Qual and JARS–Quant standards. Indicate how the qualitative and quantitative results were "mixed" or integrated (e.g., discussion; tables of joint displays; graphs; data transformation in which one form of data is transformed to the other, such as qualitative text, codes, or themes transformed into quantitative counts or variables).

- *Authors:* In mixed methods research, the findings section typically includes subsections on qualitative findings, quantitative results, and mixed methods results. This section should mirror the type of mixed methods design in terms of sequence (i.e., whether quantitative strand or qualitative strand comes first; if both are gathered at the same time, either qualitative findings or quantitative results could be presented first).
- *Reviewers:* In mixed methods Results sections (or in the Discussion section to follow), authors are conveying their mixed methods analysis through "joint display" tables or graphs that array the qualitative results next to the quantitative results (e.g., categorical or continuous data). This enables researchers to directly compare results or to see how results from the quantitative and qualitative strands were integrated.

Discussion

Discussion subsections

See the JARS–Qual and JARS–Quant standards.

- *Authors:* Typically, the Discussion section, like the Method and Findings/Results, mirrors in sequence the procedures used in the type of mixed methods design. It also reflects upon the implications of the integrated findings from across the two methods.

Note. JARS–Qual = Journal Article Reporting Standards for Qualitative Research; JARS–Quant = Journal Article Reporting Standards for Quantitative Research. Adapted from "Journal Article Reporting Standards for Qualitative Primary, Qualitative Meta-Analytic, and Mixed Methods Research in Psychology: The APA Publications and Communications Board Task Force Report," by H. M. Levitt, M. Bamberg, J. W. Creswell, D. M. Frost, R. Josselson, and C. Suárez-Orozco, 2018, *American Psychologist, 73,* pp. 41–43. Copyright 2018 by the American Psychological Association.

Table A9.2. Journal Article Reporting Standards for Quantitative Research (JARS–Quant): Information Recommended for Inclusion in Manuscripts That Report New Data Collections Regardless of Research Design

Paper section and topic	Description
Title and title page	
Title	Identify the main variables and theoretical issues under investigation and the relationships between them. Identify the populations studied.
Author note	Provide acknowledgment and explanation of any special circumstances, including • Registration information if the study has been registered • Use of data also appearing in previous publications • Prior reporting of the fundamental data in dissertations or conference papers • Sources of funding or other support • Relationships or affiliations that may be perceived as conflicts of interest • Previous (or current) affiliation of authors if different from location where study was conducted • Contact information for the corresponding author • Additional information of importance to the reader that may not be appropriately included in other sections of the paper.
Abstract	
Objectives	State the problem under investigation, including • Main hypotheses.
Participants	Describe subjects (animal research) or participants (human research), specifying their pertinent characteristics for this study; in animal research, include genus and species. Participants are described in greater detail in the body of the paper.
Method	Describe the study method, including • Research design (e.g., experiment, observational study) • Sample size • Materials used (e.g., instruments, apparatus) • Outcome measures • Data-gathering procedures, including a brief description of the source of any secondary data. If the study is a secondary data analysis, so indicate.
Findings	Report findings, including effect sizes and confidence intervals or statistical significance levels.
Conclusions	State conclusions, beyond just results, and report the implications or applications.

■ Table A9.2. (*Continued*)

Paper section and topic	Description
Introduction	
Problem	State the importance of the problem, including theoretical or practical implications.
Review of relevant scholarship	Provide a succinct review of relevant scholarship, including • Relation to previous work • Differences between the current report and earlier reports if some aspects of this study have been reported on previously.
Hypothesis, aims, and objectives	State specific hypotheses, aims, and objectives, including • Theories or other means used to derive hypotheses • Primary and secondary hypotheses • Other planned analyses. State how hypotheses and research design relate to one another.
Method	
Inclusion and exclusion	Report inclusion and exclusion criteria, including any restrictions based on demographic characteristics.
Participant characteristics	Report major demographic characteristics (e.g., age, sex, ethnicity, socioeconomic status) and important topic-specific characteristics (e.g., achievement level in studies of educational interventions). In the case of animal research, report the genus, species, and strain number or other specific identification, such as the name and location of the supplier and the stock designation. Give the number of animals and the animals' sex, age, weight, physiological condition, genetic modification status, genotype, health–immune status, drug or test naïveté (if known), and previous procedures to which the animal may have been subjected.
Sampling procedures	Describe procedures for selecting participants, including • Sampling method if a systematic sampling plan was implemented • Percentage of sample approached that actually participated • Whether self-selection into the study occurred (either by individuals or by units, such as schools or clinics) Describe settings and locations where data were collected as well as dates of data collection. Describe agreements and payments made to participants. Describe institutional review board agreements, ethical standards met, and safety monitoring.

(*table continues*)

Table A9.2. (*Continued*)

Paper section and topic	Description

Sample size, power, and precision	Describe the sample size, power, and precision, including
	• Intended sample size
	• Achieved sample size, if different from intended sample size
	• Determination of sample size, including
	  • Power analysis, or methods used to determine precision of parameter estimates
	  • Explanation of any interim analyses and stopping rules employed.

Measures and covariates	Define all primary and secondary measures and covariates, including measures collected but not included in this report.
Data collection	Describe methods used to collect data.
Quality of measurements	Describe methods used to enhance the quality of measurements, including • Training and reliability of data collectors • Use of multiple observations.
Instrumentation	Provide information on validated or ad hoc instruments created for individual studies (e.g., psychometric and biometric properties).
Masking	Report whether participants, those administering the experimental manipulations, and those assessing the outcomes were aware of condition assignments. If masking took place, provide statement regarding how it was accomplished and whether and how the success of masking was evaluated.
Psychometrics	Estimate and report reliability coefficients for the scores analyzed (i.e., the researcher's sample), if possible. Provide estimates of convergent and discriminant validity where relevant. Report estimates related to the reliability of measures, including • Interrater reliability for subjectively scored measures and ratings • Test–retest coefficients in longitudinal studies in which the retest interval corresponds to the measurement schedule used in the study • Internal consistency coefficients for composite scales in which these indices are appropriate for understanding the nature of the instruments being used in the study. Report the basic demographic characteristics of other samples if reporting reliability or validity coefficients from those samples, such as those described in test manuals or in the norming information about the instrument.

■ **Table A9.2.** (*Continued*)

Paper section and topic	Description

• Conditions and design	State whether conditions were manipulated or naturally observed. Report the type of design consistent with the JARS–Quant tables:
	• Experimental manipulation with participants randomized
	  • Table 2 and Module A
	• Experimental manipulation without randomization
	  • Table 2 and Module B
	• Clinical trial with randomization
	  • Table 2 and Modules A and C
	• Clinical trial without randomization
	  • Table 2 and Modules B and C
	• Nonexperimental design (i.e., no experimental manipulation): observational design, epidemiological design, natural history, and so forth (single-group designs or multiple-group comparisons)
	  • Table 3
	• Longitudinal design
	  • Table 4
	• *N*-of-1 studies
	  • Table 5
	• Replications
	  • Table 6
	• Report the common name given to designs not currently covered in JARS–Quant.

Data diagnostics	Describe planned data diagnostics, including • Criteria for post–data collection exclusion of participants, if any • Criteria for deciding when to infer missing data and methods used for imputation of missing data • Definition and processing of statistical outliers • Analyses of data distributions • Data transformations to be used, if any.
Analytic strategy	Describe the analytic strategy for inferential statistics and protection against experiment-wise error for • Primary hypotheses • Secondary hypotheses • Exploratory hypotheses.

(*table continues*)

Table A9.2. (*Continued*)

Paper section and topic	Description
Results	
Participant flow	Report the flow of participants, including • Total number of participants in each group at each stage of the study • Flow of participants through each stage of the study (include figure depicting flow when possible; see Figure 2).
Recruitment	Provide dates defining the periods of recruitment and repeated measures or follow-up.

Statistics and data analysis	Provide information detailing the statistical and data-analytic methods used, including
	• Missing data
	  • Frequency or percentages of missing data
	  • Empirical evidence and/or theoretical arguments for the causes of data that are missing–for example, missing completely at random, missing at random, or missing not at random
	  • Methods actually used for addressing missing data, if any
	• Description of each primary and secondary outcome, including the total sample and each subgroup, that includes the number of cases, cell means, standard deviations, and other measures that characterize the data used
	• Inferential statistics, including
	  • Results of all inferential tests conducted, including exact p values if null hypothesis statistical testing methods were used, including the minimally sufficient set of statistics (e.g., dfs, mean square [MS] effect, MS error) needed to construct the tests
	  • Effect-size estimates and confidence intervals on estimates that correspond to each inferential test conducted, when possible
	  • Clear differentiation between primary hypotheses and their tests and estimates, secondary hypotheses and their tests and estimates, and exploratory hypotheses and their tests and estimates
	• Complex data analyses—for example, structural equation modeling analyses (see Table 8), hierarchical linear models, factor analysis, multivariate analyses, and so forth, including
	  • Details of the models estimated
	  • Associated variance–covariance (or correlation) matrix or matrices

◼ **Table A9.2.** (*Continued*)

Paper section and topic	Description
	• Identification of the statistical software used to run the analyses (e.g., SAS PROC GLM, particular R library program) • Estimation problems (e.g., failure to converge, bad solution spaces), regression diagnostics, or analytic anomalies that were detected and solutions to those problems • Other data analyses performed, including adjusted analyses, indicating those that were planned and those that were not planned (though not necessarily in the level of detail of primary analyses). Report any problems with statistical assumptions and/or data distributions that could affect the validity of findings.
Discussion	
Support of original hypotheses	Provide a statement of support or nonsupport for all hypotheses, whether primary or secondary, including • Distinction by primary and secondary hypotheses • Discussion of the implications of exploratory analyses in terms of both substantive findings and error rates that may be uncontrolled.
Similarity of results	Discuss similarities and differences between reported results and the work of others.
Interpretation	Provide an interpretation of the results, taking into account • Sources of potential bias and threats to internal and statistical validity • Imprecision of measurement protocols • Overall number of tests or overlap among tests • Adequacy of sample sizes and sampling validity.
Generalizability	Discuss generalizability (external validity) of the findings, taking into account • Target population (sampling validity) • Other contextual issues (setting, measurement, time; ecological validity).
Implications	Discuss implications for future research, programs, or policy.

Note. Tables have been designed to be comprehensive and to apply widely. For any individual report, the author is expected to select the items that apply to the particular study. Adapted from "Journal Article Reporting Standards for Quantitative Research in Psychology: The APA Publications and Communications Board Task Force Report," by M. Appelbaum, H. Cooper, R. B. Kline, E. Mayo-Wilson, A. M. Nezu, and S. M. Rao, 2018, *American Psychologist, 73*, pp. 6–8. Copyright 2018 by the American Psychological Association.

10

Considering Rhetorical Style and Methodological Integrity: Troubleshooting and Tips for Publishing and Reviewing

Rhetorical style is important in reporting for the following reasons:

- If readers do not understand your approach to inquiry and your writing style is inconsistent, it will be hard for them to determine whether you have accomplished your purpose.
- If you do not understand your approach to inquiry, it will be hard for you to select what information is most important to report and to write your report in a coherent voice.

The Journal Article Reporting Standards for Qualitative Research (JARS–Qual; Levitt, Bamberg, et al., 2018) can usefully guide you as you consider how to communicate your research and report your findings. These standards focus on elements to report within your paper. Although the standards do not focus on how to design or review qualitative research, aspects of your design may influence your reporting style and also how your manuscript will be received. As discussed throughout this book, reporting qualitative research can be thought of as akin to a storytelling process. One aspect of good storytelling is to consider the various readers (e.g., fellow researchers in your field, reviewers, editors) who will be consuming your work and tailor your presentation so that they can best appreciate the work you have done (or consider telling your story to a different group!).

Although qualitative methods might be distinguished by procedures, language, and epistemological positions, there appear to be common processes that can assist

http://dx.doi.org/10.1037/0000121-010

Reporting Qualitative Research in Psychology: How to Meet APA Style Journal Article Reporting Standards, by H. M. Levitt

you as you describe how you designed your qualitative methods and that influence the review process (e.g., Elliott, Fischer, & Rennie, 1999; Levitt, Bamberg, et al., 2018; Parker, 2004; Stiles, 1993; Wertz et al., 2011; Williams & Morrow, 2009). As described earlier, the Society for Qualitative Inquiry in Psychology (Division 5 of the American Psychological Association) designated a task force of researchers to review the qualitative literature and articulate common principles for designing and evaluating qualitative research. With input from leading qualitative researchers from across a wide variety of methods and issues, they generated a paper to describe how to evaluate fidelity and utility within qualitative research in the design and review process (Levitt, Motulsky, Wertz, Morrow, & Ponterotto, 2017).

Central to this paper was the idea that evaluating research is dependent on understanding its goals, which are often informed by the tradition of inquiry in use. Because researchers can legitimately pursue research toward different ends, comprehending the purpose of their investigations is necessary when determining whether or not they have been successful in achieving it. In some of these projects, the research endeavor is seen as an attempt to reflect reality, and in others it is seen as a process that is coconstructed by researchers and participants, or that is driven by a certain theory, or in which the interpretive process is centralized.

The approach to inquiry you adopt may relate to the goal of your project. For instance, you may seek to develop a deep understanding of the way an experience is perceived, to uncover the ways systemic processes are socially constructed, to develop reliable items for a stable measure of a phenomenon, to provide guidelines that are useful for practice, or to document how discourses shift across a period of history. You can imagine the way the approach to inquiry in these research projects might differ given their varied aims, as would the language used in reporting their findings (Rennie, 1995). In some projects, findings are presented more as though anyone might arrive at them, whereas in others the process of interpretation, the theory used in developing findings, and the ways the findings were crafted by participants and researchers are a key part of the presentation.

In this chapter, I consider how these same beliefs about the inquiry process might influence your language and the arguments you craft to support your claims. This discussion builds on the explanation of traditions of inquiry described in Chapter 2 and provides some guidance for considering coherence between your reporting style and the assumptions you are making about the purpose of your research. This chapter doesn't tell you what to report; instead, it encourages you to report your research in a manner that is coherent with the epistemological assumptions you are endorsing. That is, it helps you consider your assumptions about the extent to which your perceptual limitations, worldviews, and expectations might influence the generation of your findings.

Objectivist and Constructivist Psychological Reporting

Adopt a rhetorical style that reflects

- the epistemological and methodological approaches you are using and
- an awareness of the philosophical implications of the language you are using.

When writing a qualitative report, it is important to consider how best to be conscious of the assumptions you hold about your research so that you can write in a consistent manner. Although there are variegated approaches to research reporting, I describe two dominant reporting styles that tend to intersect with researchers' approaches to inquiry. An *objectivist* rhetorical style suggests that the authors' values, beliefs, or interests do not or should not influence their findings—often reflecting a postpositive or critical realist approach to inquiry. In contrast, a *subjectivist* or *constructivist* rhetorical style suggests that findings are influenced by the authors' values, beliefs, or interests—often reflecting constructivist, critical, or social constructionist approaches to inquiry.

Although I am contrasting two positions for the purpose of sensitizing readers to the differences in style, researchers might consider how to best report their findings so that they are coherent within other epistemological perspectives or within pragmatic approaches to research. Understanding the purposes of these forms of communication across approaches can lead to bilingualism across rhetorical styles (e.g., Maxwell, 2010; McMullen, 2002). Indeed, the growing awareness that there are multiple credible traditions of inquiry has provided a foundation for the growth of qualitative research in psychology.

Objectivist Rhetoric

Objectivism is reflected in a rhetorical style in which research is reported in an impersonal manner without revealing biases or self-interest in order to convey a stance of independence between the researcher and the scientific process. It appeals to the traditions of natural science, in which researchers' expectations are not believed to influence the behavior of their subjects (i.e., inanimate entities, such as chemicals, physical objects, or gravity) and in which the objects under study do not have the capacity to deliberately vary their self-representation. Although psychology researchers at this point pretty much agree that their own perceptual limitations and expectations influence their research findings (Fine, 2013; Levitt, Surace, et al., 2018; Shadish, 1995), this style of reporting has a long history in psychology and so is often seen as convincing in our discipline. This writing tends to include minimal discussion on the influence of the researcher and focuses on demonstrating agreement with findings, regardless of the researchers' perspectives. It demonstrates an aspiration toward a neutral scientific position from which one can conduct investigation. Although there have been shifts away from an objectivist reporting style (such as allowing first-person references to the researchers), it remains the dominant reporting style in quantitative research.

Constructivist Rhetoric

Alternatives to objectivism have come from many corners of the social sciences and philosophy as its values were questioned. Instead of seeing our perspectives as scientists and the methods of inquiry we use as neutral, we increasingly recognize our perspectives as grounded in certain belief systems. Constructivist writing tends to discuss the ways in which findings developed in relation to the researchers' perspectives, cultural assumptions, and expectations. It focuses on showing how findings evolved in relation to the questions asked by the researchers, their deepening understandings, and their relationships with their participants. Qualitative researchers have questioned the wisdom of automatically writing in an objectivist tone and minimizing the appearance of researcher subjectivity rather than developing contextualized reflexive writing styles that better situate research (Gough & Madill, 2012).

Epistemologies that use constructivist rhetorical styles include social constructionist, critical, and constructivist approaches to psychology, which all question the idea that psychological knowledge is produced in value-free contexts. Social constructionist psychologists have pointed out how the understanding of our experiences is structured by social structures and systems, including the knowledge disseminated by psychological science (e.g., K. J. Gergen, 1973; Harré, 1991). Critical psychologists, led by feminist and multicultural psychologists, have made clear that our findings are culturally situated and promote sets of values at the expense of others (Hesse-Biber & Griffin, 2015; Prilleltensky, 1989; Sue & Sue, 2013). Constructivist psychologists have explored the process of how knowledge is produced and how humans generate meaning (e.g., Hardison & Neimeyer, 2012; Kelly, 1955), and psychology has learned from other disciplines to incorporate self-reflexive procedures. Qualitative methods and procedures have been adopted from sociology, philosophy, nursing, anthropology, and other social sciences and have enriched the types of research conducted in psychology.

Although there are variations in the philosophical assumptions underlying (and within) these traditions and practices, in this chapter the term *constructivism* is used to refer to the common rhetorical style across these ideologies, as it can be seen as an umbrella category in the field to reference subjectivist approaches to research. Using this reporting style, research is presented in such a manner as to acknowledge and explicitly examine how scientists shape the concepts that they use to understand the world.

Across the traditions of qualitative inquiry (i.e., postpositivist, constructivist–interpretive, critical–ideological, and pragmatic traditions), the belief that researchers come to conduct research with (and often because of) personal experiences, values, and beliefs about their subjects of inquiry is not unusual and has led to discussion of how to best present qualitative research (Rennie, 1995). This starting point challenges the dualistic participant–researcher distinction and the valuing of reporting from a purely objectivist position. Instead, qualitative reporting emphasizes a transparent discussion of the researchers' perspectives and of how they were dealt with in the analysis producing the study's results. The extent to which you emphasize these considerations in your results, though, is a matter of your own epistemological beliefs, and so it can be important to consider how you understand your own role in your research process.

How to Decide on a Reporting Style

To adopt a consistent reporting style,

■ become aware of the linguistic features of objectivist and constructivist reporting.

When developing your reporting style, you want to consider whether your research approach is more objectivist or more constructivist. Your paper will not read smoothly if, at some points in your writing, you present your results as ones that have been little influenced by your perspectives and then, at other points, you present your work in a manner that emphasizes your influence. Whatever your position, you want to make decisions that allow you to write coherently.

Features of Objectivist Reporting

First, it can be helpful to learn to recognize objectivist writing, which is the approach that most psychologists are trained in at first. Because objectivist writing is so prevalent in psychology, it can be hard to notice the features of this kind of writing. Indeed, as someone who was first trained in quantitative psychology, I find that often I slip into this form of writing as it has become natural for me. It can take some effort to become aware when I am lapsing into an objectivist rhetorical style.

When you are using objectivist reporting, you are seeking to strengthen your claims by positioning yourself as detached from or neutral in the research process. Objectivist writing tends to include the following strategies:

■ *Minimizing the focus on the investigators in your reporting or using the third person to refer to the investigators:* For instance, "The goal of this study was to examine the way students experienced praise in the context of a learning activity."
■ *Using language that suggests that findings are based in the subject of study and are external to the researcher's interpretive process:* For example, "We identified a trend in which the students evaluated praise as more sincere when it was coupled with constructive feedback, and then it led to improved performance."
■ *Using terminology that suggests that the research is accessing and depicting one real truth that exists in the world separately from its context or the investigators' position:* For example, "The findings demonstrated that students learn best in contexts of both targeted praise and criticism."

Sometimes researchers use terminology that stems from quantitative psychology to appeal to a readership that is familiar with that terminology. For instance, they may refer to the subjects they explore as *factors* or *variables*, and they might use concepts such as generalization or external validity to assess their research contribution. Because the field is in transition in terms of accepting and understanding qualitative methods and standards of reporting, qualitative researchers often need to decide whether to use terminology that is more widely understood or terminology that better reflects the approaches that they are using.

Features of Constructivist Reporting

Writing from a constructivist perspective is transparent about the role of the investigators in the research process. Researchers stress the context of their findings and work to situate the quotes, findings, and implications of their work. Constructivist writing tends to include these elements:

■ *Centralizing the investigators in your reporting of the research process:* For instance, "Driven by their classroom observations that students responded well to praise, the researchers designed the current study to examine how praise influenced students' experience of learning."
■ *Using language that makes transparent how you arrived at a conclusion:* For example, "After considering students' descriptions of the experience of praise coupled with

constructive feedback, and their repeated use of terms such as *tailored, thoughtful, caring*, and *honest*, we came to interpret the defining experience of this form of feedback as one characterized by sincerity."

■ *Using terminology that suggests that your report is describing findings that are meaningful within certain contexts and perspectives:* "We found that students' learning in public special education classes was enhanced when it occurred in a context of both targeted praise and criticism."

■ *Reporting information that better situates the investigators and describes how they dealt with their expectations in the course of a study:* For example, you may include reflections on your personal positions and characteristics relevant to the research topic (e.g., "I am a White femme lesbian researcher and have a longstanding program of research examining experiences of gender within LGBTQ [lesbian, gay, bisexual, transgender, queer and questioning] communities"); your preconceived expectations (e.g., "Although I believed that minority stressors would impact these participants, I was unsure how stigma in their communities might influence their coping"), and your efforts to set aside your beliefs so they would not influence your analysis (e.g., "I used a process of bracketing to become aware of my own preconceptions so I could attend to the experiences of my participants") or to use your perspectives in the analytic process (e.g., "I used my feminist–multicultural perspective to identify implicit sexism, heterosexism, and racism within the analysis of the narratives"). Constructivist researchers often describe tools or procedures they used to assist in this process (e.g., journaling, memoing, field notes, nonleading or open-ended questions, discussions about expectations with others). They may describe how their beliefs or values were challenged or changed in the research process. A qualitative meta-analysis of research on psychotherapy clients' experiences (Levitt, Pomerville, & Surace, 2016) found that just over 80% of the qualitative studies examined included some description of the investigators' positions and expectations or their reflexive process, or both; thus, it appears that this practice has become normative in qualitative research reporting.

■ *Describing the purpose of procedures you incorporated in your research* (see Levitt, Pomerville, Surace, & Grabowski, 2017): Researchers from more objectivist approaches tend to use mechanisms such as auditors, consensus processes, or participant feedback processes to demonstrate that multiple people can agree on an interpretation of the data—that is, to establish the objectivity of their findings. In contrast, researchers from more constructivist approaches view these procedures as valuable because they encourage awareness of how differences in perspectives influence findings and broaden the potential to consider alternative meanings or to frame meanings in light of specific perspectives or contexts.

These are elements that I see as characterizing constructivist reporting; however, the degree of emphasis on each element can vary considerably. For instance, whereas some articles might include a scant few sentences about the researchers' expectations, others might feature multiple pages describing the researchers' initial beliefs, the ways they dealt with these beliefs throughout the analysis, and the ways they were influenced in the research process. Although the trend is moving toward more constructivist reporting in qualitative research, there are a number of factors, described in the sections that follow, that you may wish to consider as you decide on your reporting style.

Deciding on a Reporting Style That Will Support Publication

To develop a reporting style that will support publication, consider

- the reporting style typically used in reporting your methodological approach,
- the tradition of inquiry that fits best with your beliefs about science, and
- the reporting style of the journal in which you are seeking to publish.

Research reports are intended to communicate to a designated audience of professionals in a given field. Added to the clarity and precision that are hallmarks of scientific writing, there is an appreciation for providing evidence that is persuasive to your select audience. Reports are published in professional journals and undergo a peer review process to evaluate their contributions. Articles in journals typically are reviewed by three experts in their field who evaluate whether articles meet these standards as well as criteria for content. For example, reviewers may check to see whether the description of research is current, whether findings communicate knowledge that moves the field forward, and whether the research is compelling.

As I have intimated, my own reporting style has continued to evolve across my career. It has changed as journals have become more accepting of articles written in a constructivist rhetorical style and permit the detailed description that qualitative Method and Results sections require. Also, I have undergone changes myself as my career developed and I shifted between researcher, reviewer, and editorial roles. The following is advice I have for you as you embark or continue on your own journey in qualitative methods.

Examine How Versions of Your Preferred Method Are Reported

As a qualitative researcher, reading writings by the originators of the qualitative methods and approaches you are considering can be illuminating. Many methods in psychology have been reshaped by researchers who hold distinctive epistemological positions (e.g., Glaser & Strauss, 1967, vs. Charmaz, 2014; Giorgi, 2009, vs. Smith, Flowers, & Larkin, 2009). They may use different procedures and language and view their research goals distinctively. By comparing their writing, you can see what style works best for you.

Read About Traditions of Inquiry in Psychological Research

Reading works by qualitative methodologists can assist you in deciding which perspectives fit best with you. A variety of schemes have been used to categorize epistemological positions and to consider how they influence the research process (e.g., Guba & Lincoln, 2005; Levitt, Motulsky, et al., 2017; Madill & Gough, 2008; Parker, 2004; Ponterotto, 2005b). This is a fascinating literature and can liberate you to make decisions about your own approach to research. Knowing the beliefs that you hold dear about the research endeavor can help you make decisions about the processes you would like to use to honor them. It can inform where you wish to publish and can enable you to communicate clearly about the legitimacy of your epistemological approach during the writing, review, and publication process.

Read Qualitative Research in the Journals in Which You Wish to Publish

Whatever your own beliefs might be, you might wish to publish in a journal that has a readership or editors who hold a different set of assumptions and beliefs. Whereas some journals are used to publishing qualitative research and hold standards that are in keeping with the logic of these approaches, others may not have editorial staff or practices that are informed about qualitative methods. (Keep in mind that editors may change, and so you want to look at editorial policies and issues published under the editor to whom you would be submitting your work.) They may not know how to review qualitative research or may use reporting styles that are based erroneously on quantitative research traditions. I have found it helpful to be aware of the reporting practices in journals when I submit a paper. There are a number of ways in which this awareness can help you:

- You might decide to change your style of reporting to accommodate the perspective of the journal and appeal to the epistemological beliefs of your readers (its editors, reviewers, and consumers).
- You might decide to retain your style but to add into your text justifications or descriptions that allow the logic that you are using to become intelligible to your readers. You can present your reporting style as legitimate and cite others who have elaborated the tradition you are using.
- You might decide to use the review process as an opportunity to educate reviewers or editors about your reporting style. Knowing more about a journal's past publications can inform you about its editors' and reviewers' level of receptivity to and knowledge about qualitative research. The next section of this chapter discusses actions you might take along these lines.

Submitting to journals that are not familiar with qualitative research or with the method or tradition of inquiry you are using is not always a bad idea. Although you may be met with a rejection when a journal is not prepared for reviewing qualitative research (and so you might weigh into your decision how an extra delay of a few months might influence your goals), at times the risk is worthwhile. It can open up a new outlet for publishing your research and allow your research to reach a new audience. It can encourage journals to recruit editors or reviewers who are educated in these methods and able to competently review them. Also, it can enter you into a dialogue about methods with colleagues in your field that might be beneficial in many ways. The section that follows focuses on this exchange.

Communicating With Journals

When communicating with journals about publishing qualitative research,

- include information about your method in your cover letter to the editor;
- be prepared to educate editors and reviewers about your methodological approach; and
- make clear the basis for the methodological integrity of your work in your paper, cover letter, and response to requests for revisions.

With the advent of the Society for Qualitative Inquiry in Psychology (SQIP) recommendations for designing and reviewing qualitative methods (Levitt, Motulsky, et al., 2017), the JARS–Qual guidelines, a film on reviewing qualitative research available on the American Psychological Association Continuing Education website (American Psychological Association, 2016), and a plethora of writings on qualitative research methods, journal editors and reviewers have a rich set of resources to support their process of reviewing manuscripts. The following are ideas to consider when submitting articles or responding to requests for revisions that can aid you in the publication process.

Include Information About Your Method in Your Cover Letter

Especially when first submitting research to a journal that does not specialize in qualitative research, it can be helpful to include a note in your cover letter to make clear both the method and the tradition of inquiry you are using (e.g., critical research, constructivist qualitative research) and to explicitly request reviewers who use a similar approach. Typically, editors seek out reviewers who have expertise in the method used in the study as well as the content area, and so this statement will draw their attention to your method. Also, you can state in your note that you have followed the JARS–Qual guidelines in order to affirm that your work is being presented within accepted professional standards. In addition, you might state why you think your work is a strong fit for that journal, perhaps citing research you have already published in that journal or describing how your work fits with the journal's mission statement (typically on their website). Many journals ask authors to nominate reviewers, so it can be helpful to select reviewers with expertise in your method as well as your topic. If the journal process allows, it is helpful to indicate to the journal editor the basis of expertise of the editors you suggest.

Educate Editors and Reviewers About Your Method and Approach

No journal editor can be expected to have expertise in every research method and approach. Because of this impossibility, journals often have associate or consulting editors who assist in reviewing manuscripts outside of the editor's area of expertise. When I am acting as an editor, I find that I learn about research methods through the reviews I manage. Both reviewers and authors have shared information with me that has allowed me to assess papers more fairly, and I appreciate learning from both sides. As an author, I find that looking at the review process as a chance to shape the field by communicating my perspectives to reviewers and editors is helpful. If I can educate reviewers and editors about qualitative methods, then I am having an impact beyond the scope of my own single article. Until recently, it has been through this process that I feel I can advocate most for qualitative research. Also, it can be empowering to reframe the review process as one of dialogue and mutual learning.

Make Clear the Basis for Methodological Integrity in Your Communications

You can state in your cover letter, as well as in your paper itself, the strengths of your paper in terms of its methodological integrity. Presenting your paper as analysis that has used rigorous methods might assist editors who are not familiar with qualitative methods to better recognize the strengths of your work. In addition, you can use the framework of methodological integrity to argue for the strengths of your article. Indeed, the SQIP recommendations (Levitt, Motulsky, et al., 2017) include principles that were deliberately written to provide tips for authors and reviewers when negotiating the review process. Many of these tips can be recruited as arguments to help justify sound methodological choices within a review process that might be less traditional or more tailored to the characteristics of the individual study. The recommendations make available many of the arguments that I and other members of the SQIP task force have used to rebut the more common problematic review comments we have encountered.

Future Directions for Qualitative Reporting Standards

The incorporation of reporting standards for qualitative research has marked a new era for our discipline. JARS–Qual provides guidance for researchers who are seeking to submit qualitative research to journals as well as for editors and reviewers who are evaluating those submissions. It is an important step toward not only greater methodological sophistication but also an embrace of pluralistic approaches to psychological research methods and epistemologies.

Flexible Reporting Standards to Support Innovation and Tailoring to Increase Methodological Integrity

The JARS–Qual guidelines were developed deliberately to provide a flexible structure to support writings using a wide variety of research methods and traditions of inquiry. Openness in writing style can allow researchers to explore metaphors and find modes of presentation that challenge boundaries (Richardson, 1994). JARS–Qual permits flexibility by considering common features that strengthen the intelligibility across qualitative reporting rather than prescribing rigid section formats. Basing the standards on common processes has had a number of advantages:

- It prevents the foreclosure of the field on specific qualitative methods, which might prohibit the innovation of new methods such as the burgeoning artistic research tradition (Bhattacharya & Payne, 2016; M. M. Gergen & Gergen, 2012).
- It permits researchers to tailor set methods and traditions of inquiry to the specific research questions they wish to explore and the characteristics of their individual studies.
- It encourages an understanding of the logic beneath qualitative methods reporting rather than prescribing a checklist of items that do not bend to the traditions and issues under exploration.
- The tailoring of designs maximizes methodological integrity, whereas a more rigid approach to identifying only certain designs would constrain it.

A positive aspect of the JARS–Qual Working Group was that we came together with a sense of valuing the perspectives and ideas of others and an interest in generating standards that would work for the field. Although I expect that future iterations of the reporting standards will continue to improve the work we have conducted, I hope that the standards continue to be crafted in such a way that they can work within multiple epistemological perspectives and goals. As a group, we continued to remind ourselves to maintain openness to the diversity of methodological perspectives and traditions that exist in our field and to avoid privileging our own perspectives. I hope that any lapses in our work are corrected over time, and I encourage a strong interest in both methodological and epistemological diversity with involvement from people with expertise across a range of these traditions.

In terms of the future development of the field of qualitative psychology research, we need to strive to protect diversity and pluralism in terms of methods and epistemologies. If we wish to be complex thinkers, I believe it is helpful to understand not only our own theories but also competing theories. Learning about other perspectives allows us to better see our own limits and advantages as well as appreciate those of others. We can learn by seeking the complementariness across approaches as well as by seeking to understand why differences exist and how they function. (To me, this practice extends beyond our research approaches to our investments in many aspects of our lives, including our research areas, psychotherapy orientations, cultures, and identities.) To advance the reporting of qualitative methods, we need to continue to educate students to value diversity and to appreciate different perspectives with depth. This means that we need to create structural supports to encounter other ways of thinking that may be less familiar, such as coursework, modeling, mentors, and research apprenticeship opportunities.

Changing Receptivity

While making decisions about your reporting style, it can be helpful to keep in mind that receptivity to qualitative research has been improving in psychology. Granting agencies are increasingly demanding mixed methods research to increase the integrity of research being conducted (e.g., Creswell, Klassen, Clark, & Smith, 2011). In a recent qualitative study, leading quantitative and qualitative researchers were found to be skeptical of naive objectivity as the aim of scientific methods. Instead, they tended to see the goal of science as the convergence of findings across multiple sets of researchers and methods (Levitt, Surace, et al., 2018). From this perspective, science is most strengthened when both qualitative and quantitative researchers work together to develop knowledge on which they can agree.

There appears to be a divergence, though, between the opinions held by leading methodologists and the types of information being shared at introductory levels of training. In Eagly and Riger's (2014) review of 10 popular psychology methods textbooks, they found only one discussion and one mention of epistemology. They called for more in-depth discussion of both qualitative methods and epistemological issues at the introductory level so students can begin psychological research with a more realistic science education. Greater attention to qualitative methods in both undergraduate and graduate research classes is necessary.

Education on Qualitative Research

As the demand for qualitative research has grown at the professional level, training on qualitative methods in graduate education has increased as well (Ponterotto, 2005a). Journals that have the expertise to evaluate qualitative research are expanding. In addition to learning about reporting standards, researchers are encouraged to learn more about the methods and procedures they would like to use and to seek out supervision as they embark on the process of conducting qualitative research. Just as psychologists take courses in statistics and seek supervision to support their initial quantitative analyses, similar processes are needed to advance the development of qualitative researchers. And just as reviewers of quantitative research are expected to have met these requirements and to have a history of conducting quantitative research themselves, journal reviewers and editors should seek appropriate levels of expertise for qualitative research. The process of embracing qualitative methods in psychology has been gradual, as many editors and reviewers were educated before qualitative methods coursework was available in graduate training. As training in qualitative methods increases and becomes an expected part of methods education, though, increasing numbers of reviewers with expertise in qualitative and mixed methods research continue to become available (see Rubin, Bell, & McClelland, 2017, for educational recommendations).

Also, as the JARS–Qual guidelines assist journals to become acquainted with qualitative methods reporting and accustomed to qualitative reporting, this already advancing process is poised to increase in pace. An important shift is that the standards deliberately make room for a variety of epistemological approaches, encouraging the acceptance of multiple traditions of inquiry, greater rhetorical flexibility, and the continued development of qualitative traditions. As pluralistic approaches to methods expand, so will the valuing of the many tools and perspectives we can bring to the research endeavor and our very vision of science.

APPENDIX
Abstracts of the 15 Articles Used as Examples in Text

Health Psychology
2015, Vol. 34, No. 4, 314–327

Responsible Men, Blameworthy Women: Black Heterosexual Men's Discursive Constructions of Safer Sex and Masculinity

Lisa Bowleg, Andrea L. Heckert, Tia L. Brown, and Jenné S. Massie
The George Washington University

Objective: Although Black heterosexual men (BHM) in the United States rank among those most affected by HIV, research about how safer sex messages shape their safer sex behaviors is rare, highlighting the need for innovative qualitative methodologies such as critical discursive psychology (CDP). This CDP study examined how (a) BHM construct safer sex and masculinity; (b) BHM positioned themselves in relation to conventional masculinity; and (c) discursive context (individual interview vs. focus group) shaped talk about safer sex and masculinity. *Method:* Data included individual interviews ($n = 30$) and 4 focus groups ($n = 26$) conducted with 56 self-identified Black/African American heterosexual men, ages 18 to 44. *Results:* Analyses highlighted 5 main constructions: (a) condoms as signifiers of "safe" women; (b) blaming women for STI/responsibility for safer sex; (c) relationship/trust/knowledge; (d) condom mandates; and (e) public health safer sex. Discourses positioned BHM in terms of conventional masculinity when talk denied men's agency for safer sex and/or contraception, or positioned women as deceitful, or apathetic about sexual risk and/or pregnancy. Notably, discourses also spotlighted alternative masculinities relevant to taking responsibility for safer sex or sexual exclusivity. Discursive context, namely the homosocial nature of focus group discussions, shaped how participants conversed about safer sex, and masculinity but not the content of that talk. *Conclusion:* In denying BHM's responsibility for safer sex, BHM's discourses about safer sex and masculinity often mirror public health messages, underscoring a critical need to sync these discourses to reduce sexual risk, and develop gender-transformative safer sex interventions for BHM.

Keywords: critical discursive psychology, safer sex, masculinity, Black men, homosociality

Journal of Counseling Psychology
2017, Vol. 64, No. 2, 192–205

The Complexities of Power in Feminist Multicultural Psychotherapy Supervision

Alexis V. Arczynski
University of Oklahoma

Susan L. Morrow
University of Utah

The goal of the present study was to understand how current feminist multicultural supervisors understand and implement their feminist multicultural principles into clinical supervision. We addressed this aim by answering the following research question: How do self-identified feminist multicultural psychotherapy supervisors conceptualize and practice feminist supervision that is explicitly multicultural? The perspectives of 14 participant supervisors were obtained by using semistructured initial interviews, follow-up interviews, and feedback interviews and were investigated via a feminist constructivist grounded theory design and analysis. Most participants identified as counseling psychologists ($n = 12$), women ($n = 11$) and temporarily able-bodied ($n = 11$); but they identified with diverse racial/ethnic, sexual, spiritual/religious, generational, and nationality statuses. A 7-category empirical framework emerged that explained how the participants anticipated and managed power in supervision. The core category, the complexities of power in supervision, explained how participants conceptualized power in supervisory relationships. The 6 remaining categories were bringing history into the supervision room, creating trust through openness and honesty, using a collaborative process, meeting shifting developmental (a)symmetries, cultivating critical reflexivity, and looking at and counterbalancing the impact of context. Limitations of the study, implications for research, and suggestions to use the theoretical framework to transform supervisory practice and training are discussed.

Public Significance Statement
The results of the present study revealed that the strategies employed by self-identified feminist multicultural supervisors were used to anticipate and manage power within and external to the supervisory triad. The strategies, use of historical and social contexts, reflexivity, and developmental attunement, were used via transparency and collaboration, were subsumed under the mantle of power and served to reconfigure good supervision practices.

Keywords: psychotherapy supervision, multiculturalism, feminism, counseling psychology, qualitative research

Psychotherapy
2016, Vol. 53, No. 1, 78–89

The Journey of an Integrationist: A Grounded Theory Analysis

Tomas Rihacek and Ester Danelova
Masaryk University

Surveys among psychotherapists tend to show a high preference for integrationism/eclecticism. There is, however, a lack of empirical studies exploring the process by which these psychotherapists arrive at this orientation. To answer this question, 22 autobiographies published by integrative psychotherapists were analyzed using grounded theory analytic procedures. The analysis resulted in a 3-stage developmental model, consisting of (a) the Adherence Phase, (b) the Destabilization Phase, and (c) the Consolidation Phase. The results are discussed in relation to several speculative models of psychotherapist development toward integration, as well as empirical literature on psychotherapist development. The results suggest that the tendency toward integration is best regarded as a natural part of the process of psychotherapist development.

Keywords: psychotherapy integration, psychotherapist development, personal psychotherapeutic approach, grounded theory

Journal of Family Psychology
2011, Vol. 25, No. 1, 1–10

Stigma and Intimacy in Same-Sex Relationships: A Narrative Approach

David M. Frost
San Francisco State University

Lesbian, gay, and bisexual individuals in romantic relationships experience stigma, prejudice, and discrimination stemming from widespread social devaluation of same-sex relationships. Research on same-sex couples has demonstrated a negative association between experiences of stigma and relationship quality. However, critical questions remain unanswered regarding how experiences of stigma become more or less meaningful within the context of same-sex relationships. This paper presents a study of the stories that a purposive sample of 99 individuals in same-sex relationships wrote about their relational high points, low points, decisions, and goals, as well as their experiences of stigma directly related to their relationships. Narrative analysis of these stories revealed that participants utilized several psychological strategies for making meaning of their experiences of stigma within the context of their relationships. Some participants framed stigma as having a negative impact on their relationships, while others framed stigma as relevant, but external to their lives. Some participants saw stigma as providing an opportunity to (re)define notions of commitment and relational legitimacy. Additionally, many participants framed stigma as bringing them closer to their partners and strengthening the bond within their relationships. The results of this study illuminate the psychological strategies individuals in same-sex couples use to make meaning of, cope with, and overcome societal devaluation thereby furthering understandings of the association between stigma and intimacy within marginalized relationships.

Keywords: relationships, narrative, stigma, minority stress, intimacy

Health Psychology
2015, Vol. 34, No. 4, 407–416

Chronotope Disruption as a Sensitizing Concept for Understanding Chronic Illness Narratives

Tim Gomersall
University of Sheffield

Anna Madill
University of Leeds

Objectives: This article aims to elaborate chronotope disruption —a changed relation to time and space— as a sensitizing concept for understanding chronic illness narratives. *Method:* Sixteen men and 16 women with Type 2 diabetes were purposefully sampled. Each was interviewed about his or her experience of diabetes self-management using the biographical-narrative interview method. Transcripts were inspected for key moments defined as emotionally laden stories relevant to the purpose of the research. We present dialogically inflected discursive analysis of exemplar extracts. *Results:* The analysis demonstrates how the concept of chronotope disruption helps identify, and understand, important aspects of patients' chronic illness narratives. First, we investigate how medical advice can conflict with embodied experience and how progressive bodily deterioration can provoke a reevaluation of past illness (self-mis)management. Second, the increasing temporal and spatial intrusion of chronic illness into participants' lives is examined. Finally, we focus on the masquerade of health as an attempt to manage, hide, or deny that one is physically challenged. *Conclusions:* Chronotope disruption offers a useful sensitizing concept for approaching chronic illness narratives and around which to organize analytical insights and to develop practice. Chronotope analysis fills an important gap in the science through compensating current health sciences' focus on rationality, cognition, and *prospective* time (prediction) with a patient-oriented focus on emotionality, embodiment, and *retrospective* time (nostalgia). Chronotope disruption could be used to develop practice by gaining empathic understanding of patients' life-worlds and provides a tool to examine how new technologies change the way in which the chronically ill have "being" in the world.

Keywords: diabetes, self-management, illness narratives, qualitative methods, chronotope

Journal of Consulting and Clinical Psychology
2007, Vol. 75, No. 6, 875–887

Emotional Processing in Experiential Therapy: Why "the Only Way Out Is Through"

Antonio Pascual-Leone
University of Windsor

Leslie S. Greenberg
York University

The purpose of this study was to examine observable moment-by-moment steps in emotional processing as they occurred within productive sessions of experiential therapy. Global distress was identified as an unprocessed emotion with high arousal and low meaningfulness. The investigation consisted of 2 studies as part of a task analysis that examined clients processing distress in live video-recorded therapy sessions. Clients in both studies were adults in experiential therapy for depression and ongoing interpersonal problems. Study 1 was the discovery-oriented phase of task analysis, which intensively examined 6 examples of global distress. The qualitative findings produced a model showing: global distress, fear, shame, and aggressive anger as undifferentiated and insufficiently processed emotions; the articulation of needs and negative self-evaluations as a pivotal step in change; and assertive anger, self-soothing, hurt, and grief as states of advanced processing. Study 2 tested the model using a sample of 34 clients in global distress. A multivariate analysis of variance showed that the model of emotional processing predicted positive in-session effects, and bootstrapping analyses were used to demonstrate that distinct emotions emerged moment by moment in predicted sequential patterns.

Keywords: emotional processing, emotion-focused therapy, distress, task analysis, change mechanisms

Journal of Counseling Psychology
2011, Vol. 58, No. 2, 210–221

Sexual Orientation Microaggressions: The Experience of Lesbian, Gay, Bisexual, and Queer Clients in Psychotherapy

Kimber Shelton and Edward A. Delgado-Romero
University of Georgia

Psychological research has shown the detrimental effects that overt heterosexism have on lesbian, gay, bisexual, and queer (LGBQ) clients and on the psychotherapeutic relationship. However, the effects of subtle forms of discrimination, specifically sexual orientation microaggressions, have on LGBQ clients and the therapeutic relationship have not been addressed. This study used qualitative methodology to explore the phenomenon of sexual orientation microaggressions with 16 self-identified LGBQ psychotherapy clients. Results of this study support the existence of sexual orientation microaggressions within the therapeutic environment and provide a descriptive account of 7 sexual orientation microaggression themes, channels of microaggression communication, and the impact microaggressions have on therapy and clients.

Keywords: sexual orientation microaggressions; psychotherapy with lesbian, gay, bisexual, and queer clients; covert heterosexism

Health Psychology
2017, Vol. 36, No. 2, 143–151

The Psychological Challenges of Living With an Ileostomy:
An Interpretative Phenomenological Analysis

Jonathan A. Smith
Birkbeck, University of London

Johanna Spiers
University of Hull

Phillip Simpson
York Teaching Hospital, York, United Kingdom

Adam R. Nicholls
University of Hull

Objectives: Ileostomy, in which the small intestine is redirected out of an abdominal wall so that waste is collected using a bag, is used to treat conditions including inflammatory bowel disease and colorectal cancer. This article reports an in-depth idiographic analysis of the experience of living with an ileostomy. *Method:* Twenty-one participants took part in semistructured interviews about their lives and relationships. Those interviews were transcribed verbatim and analyzed using the experiential qualitative methodology interpretative phenomenological analysis. *Results:* Two superordinate themes arose from the data: ileostomy's intrapersonal impact and the impact of ileostomy on relationships with others. The authors found that ileostomy may destabilize the sense of self, disrupt body image, and alter experience of age and sexuality. Other participants were able to use their illness to positively reframe the self. Disclosure of ileostomy status was difficult for some. Intimate and friend relationships were often challenged by stoma status, whereas other family relationships were largely characterized as supportive. *Conclusions:* Ileostomy may impact upon both intra- and interpersonal aspects of the lives of those who live with it, in both negative and positive ways. Consequently, the sense of self can appear challenged, and relationships with partners, family members and friendships could be causes of distress. On the other hand, some partners were supportive, and children were found to be sources of comfort.

Keywords: ileostomy, phenomenology, qualitative, relationships, self

Supplemental materials: http://dx.doi.org/10.1037/hea0000427.supp

Rehabilitation Psychology
2014, Vol. 59, No. 4, 386–398

Work-Related Social Skills:
Definitions and Interventions in Public Vocational Rehabilitation

Brian N. Phillips and Ashley A. Kaseroff
University of Wisconsin-Madison

Allison R. Fleming
University of Kentucky

Garrett E. Huck
University of Wisconsin-Madison

Objective: Social skills play an important role in employment. This study provides a qualitative analysis of salient work-related social skills and interventions for addressing social skills in public vocational rehabilitation (VR). *Research Design:* A modified consensual qualitative research (CQR) approach was taken to understand the elements and influence of work related social skills in public VR. Thirty-five counselors, supervisors, and administrators participated in semistructured interviews to provide their perspectives of work-related social skills and the interventions they use for addressing these skills. *Results:* Multiple aspects of work-related social skills were described as being important for VR consumer success. The most common work-related social skills across all participants were nonverbal communication and the ability to connect with others. Primary social interventions included informal social skills training (SST), systems collaboration, and creating an appropriate job match. *Conclusions:* Public rehabilitation agency staff, constantly faced with addressing work-related social skills, possess many insights about salient skills and interventions that can benefit future research and practice. Agencies currently address social skills deficits by providing interventions to both person and environment. The research provides directions for future research related to identification of social skills and interventions to address related deficits.

Keywords: social skills, social skills training, vocational rehabilitation, rehabilitation counseling

Professional Psychology: Research and Practice
2006, Vol. 37, No. 4, 359–366

Listening to Parents' Voices: Participatory Action Research in the Schools

Christine J. Ditrano
Rockland County Board of Cooperative Educational Services

Louise Bordeaux Silverstein
Yeshiva University

How can schools and parents work together more effectively? This article describes a participatory action research (PAR) project with a group of parents whose children had been classified as having emotional disabilities. As the parents shared their stories of trying to navigate the special education system, they developed critical consciousness about their experiences of stress, powerlessness, and alienation. They became mobilized and obtained information about testing, diagnostic classification, and educational options for their children. Armed with this information, they developed and implemented an action plan to improve family–school relationships at the local, community, and state levels. The article concludes with an example of how the PAR model can be exported to a variety of mental health settings.

Keywords: qualitative research, participatory action research, family–school collaboration

Psychological Bulletin
2016, Vol. 142, No. 8, 801–830

A Qualitative Meta-Analysis Examining Clients' Experiences of Psychotherapy: A New Agenda

Heidi M. Levitt
University of Massachusetts Boston

Andrew Pomerville
University of Michigan

Francisco I. Surace
University of Massachusetts Boston

This article argues that psychotherapy practitioners and researchers should be informed by the substantive body of qualitative evidence that has been gathered to represent clients' own experiences of therapy. The current meta-analysis examined qualitative research studies analyzing clients' experiences within adult individual psychotherapy that appeared in English-language journals. This omnibus review integrates research from across psychotherapy approaches and qualitative methods, focusing on the cross-cutting question of how clients experience therapy. It utilized an innovative method in which 67 studies were subjected to a grounded theory meta-analysis in order to develop a hierarchy of data and then 42 additional studies were added into this hierarchy using a content meta-analytic method—summing to 109 studies in total. Findings highlight the critical psychotherapy experiences for clients, based upon robust findings across these research studies. Process-focused principles for practice are generated that can enrich therapists' understanding of their clients in key clinical decision-making moments. Based upon these findings, an agenda is suggested in which research is directed toward heightening therapists' understanding of clients and recognizing them as agents of change within sessions, supporting the client as self-healer paradigm. This research aims to improve therapists' sensitivity to clients' experiences and thus can expand therapists' attunement and intentionality in shaping interventions in accordance with whichever theoretical orientation is in use. The article advocates for the full integration of the qualitative literature in psychotherapy research in which variables are conceptualized in reference to an understanding of clients' experiences in sessions.

Keywords: psychotherapy, qualitative study, psychotherapy clients, metasynthesis, meta-analysis

Health Psychology
2015, Vol. 34, No. 4, 381–397

Reducing Youth Screen Time: Qualitative Metasynthesis of Findings on Barriers and Facilitators

Karl E. Minges
Yale University

Neville Owen
Baker IDI Heart and Diabetes Institute, Melbourne, Australia,
and University of Melbourne

Jo Salmon
Deakin University

Ariana Chao
Yale University

David W. Dunstan
Baker IDI Heart and Diabetes Institute, Melbourne, Australia,
and Monash University

Robin Whittemore
Yale University

Objective: An integrated perspective on the relevant qualitative findings on the experience of screen time in youth can inform the development of hypotheses to be tested in future research and can guide the development of interventions to decrease sedentary behavior. The purpose of this qualitative metasynthesis was to explore parent, youth, and educational professionals' perceptions of barriers to, and facilitators of, reducing youth screen time. *Method:* Qualitative metasynthesis techniques were used to analyze and synthesize 15 qualitative studies of screen time among youth (11–18 years) meeting inclusion criteria. The phrases, quotes, and/or author interpretations (i.e., theme or subtheme) were recorded in a data display matrix to facilitate article comparisons. Codes were collapsed into 23 categories of similar conceptual meaning and 3 overarching themes were derived using thematic analysis procedures. *Results:* Study sample sizes ranged from 6 to 270 participants from 6 countries. Data collection methods included focus groups ($n = 6$), interviews ($n = 4$), focus groups and interviews ($n = 4$), and naturalistic observation ($n = 1$) with youth and/or parents. Data analysis techniques included thematic analysis ($n = 9$), content analysis ($n = 3$), grounded theory ($n = 1$), observation ($n = 1$), and interpretive phenomenological analysis ($n = 1$). Three thematic categories were identified: (a) youth's norms—screen time is an integral part of daily life, and facilitates opportunities for entertainment, social interaction, and escapism; (b) family dynamics and parental roles—parents are conflicted and send mixed messages about the appropriate uses and amounts of screen time; and, (c) resources and environment—engagement in screen time is dependent on school, community, neighborhood, and home environmental contexts. *Conclusions:* Screen time is an established norm in many youth cultures, presenting barriers to behavior change. Parents recognize the importance of reducing youth screen time, but model and promote engagement themselves. For youth and parents, mutually agreed rules, limits, and parental monitoring of screen time were perceived as likely to be effective.

Keywords: television time, sedentary behavior, youth, qualitative, review

Journal of Counseling Psychology
2009, Vol. 56, No. 4, 521–536

Making Cross-Racial Therapy Work: A Phenomenological Study of Clients' Experiences of Cross-Racial Therapy

Doris F. Chang and Alexandra Berk
New School for Social Research

A phenomenological and consensual qualitative study of clients' lived experiences of cross-racial therapy was conducted to enhance the understanding of whether, how, and under what conditions race matters in the therapy relationship. The sample consisted of 16 racial and/or ethnic minority clients who received treatment from 16 White, European American therapists across a range of treatment settings. Participants who reported a satisfying experience of cross-racial therapy ($n = 8$) were examined in relation to gender-matched controls and, in most cases, race/ethnicity-matched controls ($n = 8$) who reported an overall unsatisfying experience. Therapy satisfaction was assessed during the screening process and was confirmed during the research interview. Therapy narratives were analyzed with consensual qualitative research to identify client, therapist, and relational factors that distinguished satisfied participants from unsatisfied participants. Findings reveal substantial differences at the level of individual characteristics and relational processes, providing evidence of both universal (etic) as well as culture- or context-specific (emic) aspects of healing relationships. Recommendations for facilitating positive alliance formation in cross-racial therapy are provided, based on clients' descriptions of facilitative conditions in the therapy relationship.

Keywords: racial/ethnic matching, psychotherapy, therapeutic alliance, phenomenology

Rehabilitation Psychology
2013, Vol. 58, No. 4, 377–385

Accessing Crisis Intervention Services After Brain Injury: A Mixed Methods Study

Cara Meixner and Cynthia R. O'Donoghue
James Madison University

Michelle Witt
Crossroads to Brain Injury Recovery, Inc., Harrisonburg, Virginia

Purpose: To understand empirically the perceived barriers to accessing crisis intervention services for individuals with acquired brain injury. *Method:* This action research design encompassed 2 phases of mixed methods data collection and analysis. Phase 1 consisted of the electronic distribution of a survey comprised primarily of quantitative items, launched to a nonrandom sample of 226 providers with a response rate of 49% ($n = 110$). Phase 2 entailed 7 focus group interviews with 25 participants, designed to add explanatory power to Phase 1 results. *Results:* Quantitative results revealed an array of major barriers significant to persons with brain injury, such as funding for services, coexisting diagnoses, and limited self-advocacy. Organizationally specific barriers included funding for services, limited training and education, and systems resources (e.g., personnel). Adding depth and insight, qualitative findings triangulated with these results, also highlighting the prevalence of the funding barrier and pointing to additional barriers relative to the individual, the family, and external stigma. *Conclusions:* The need for convenient, cost-effective, and applicable training and education is paramount. Opportunities for interagency cross training and education, particularly around risk assessment, psychosocial adjustment symptoms, and the biomechanical causes of psychiatric symptoms may alleviate perceived disconnections, improve provider confidence, and mitigate crises. Developing interprofessional teams of providers to maximize access to services, either face-to-face or virtual, is integral. These perspectives highlight opportunities to improve access to services and to strengthen relationships across providers and agencies.

Keywords: brain injury, access, barriers, crisis, mixed methods

Developmental Psychology
2010, Vol. 46, No. 3, 602–618

© 2010 American Psychological Association
0012-1649/10/$12.00   http://dx.doi.org/10.1037/a0018201

Academic Trajectories of Newcomer Immigrant Youth

Carola Suárez-Orozco
New York University and Institute for Advanced Study,
Princeton, New Jersey

Francisco X. Gaytán
Northeastern Illinois University

Hee Jin Bang
William T. Grant Foundation, New York, New York

Juliana Pakes
Harvard University

Erin O'Connor
New York University

Jean Rhodes
University of Massachusetts, Boston

Immigration to the United States presents both challenges and opportunities that affect students' academic achievement. Using a 5-year longitudinal, mixed methods approach, we identified varying academic trajectories of newcomer immigrant students from Central America, China, the Dominican Republic, Haiti, and Mexico. Latent class growth curve analysis revealed that although some newcomer students performed at high or improving levels over time, others showed diminishing performance. Multinomial logistic regressions identified significant group differences in academic trajectories, particularly between the high-achieving youth and the other groups. In keeping with ecological–developmental and stage–environment fit theories, School Characteristics (school segregation rate, school poverty rate, and student perceptions of school violence), Family Characteristics (maternal education, parental employment, and household structure), and Individual Characteristics (academic English proficiency, academic engagement, psychological symptoms, gender, and 2 age-related risk factors, number of school transitions and being overaged for grade placement) were associated with different trajectories of academic performance. A series of case studies triangulate many of the quantitative findings as well as illuminate patterns that were not detected in the quantitative data. Thus, the mixed methods approach sheds light on the cumulative developmental challenges that immigrant students face as they adjust to their new educational settings.

Keywords: immigrants, adolescence, academic trajectories, mixed methods

Supplemental materials: http://dx.doi.org/10.1037/a0018201.supp

References

American Psychological Association. (2010). *Publication manual of the American Psychological Association* (6th ed.). Washington, DC: Author.

American Psychological Association. (Producer). (2016). *How to review qualitative research* [Video file]. Available from http://www.apa.org/pubs/journals/resources/review-manuscript-ce-video.aspx

Angus, L. E., & McLeod, J. (2004). *The handbook of narrative and psychotherapy: Practice, theory, and research*. Thousand Oaks, CA: Sage. http://dx.doi.org/10.4135/9781412973496

Appelbaum, M., Cooper, H., Kline, R. B., Mayo-Wilson, E., Nezu, A. M., & Rao, S. M. (2018). Journal article reporting standards for quantitative research in psychology: The APA Publications and Communications Board task force report. *American Psychologist, 73*, 3–25. http://dx.doi.org/10.1037/amp0000191

Arczynski, A. V., & Morrow, S. L. (2017). The complexities of power in feminist multicultural psychotherapy supervision. *Journal of Counseling Psychology, 64*, 192–205. http://dx.doi.org/10.1037/cou0000179

Bamberg, M. (2012). Narrative analysis. In H. Cooper, P. M. Camic, D. L. Long, A. T. Panter, D. Rindskopf, & K. Sher (Eds.), *APA handbook of research methods in psychology* (Vol. 2, pp. 85–102). Washington, DC: American Psychological Association.

Bamberg, M., & Georgakopoulou, A. (2008). Small stories as a new perspective in narrative and identity analysis. *Text & Talk, 28*, 377–396. http://dx.doi.org/10.1515/TEXT.2008.018

Bhattacharya, K., & Payne, R. (2016). Mixing mediums, mixing selves: Arts-based contemplative approaches to border crossings. *International Journal of Qualitative Studies in Education, 29*, 1100–1117. http://dx.doi.org/10.1080/09518398.2016.1201163

Bowleg, L., Heckert, A. L., Brown, T. L., & Massie, J. S. (2015). Responsible men, blameworthy women: Black heterosexual men's discursive constructions of safer sex and masculinity. *Health Psychology, 34*, 314–327. http://dx.doi.org/10.1037/hea0000216

Braun, V., & Clarke, V. (2006). Using thematic analysis in psychology. *Qualitative Research in Psychology, 3*, 77–101. http://dx.doi.org/10.1191/1478088706qp063oa

Bruner, J. S. (1990). *Acts of meaning*. Cambridge, MA: Harvard University Press.

Bryant, A., & Charmaz, K. (Eds.). (2010). *The Sage handbook of grounded theory*. Thousand Oaks, CA: Sage.

Castro, F. G., & Coe, K. (2007). Traditions and alcohol use: A mixed-methods analysis. *Cultural Diversity & Ethnic Minority Psychology, 13*, 269–284. http://dx.doi.org/10.1037/1099-9809.13.4.269

Chang, D. F., & Berk, A. (2009). Making cross-racial therapy work: A phenomenological study of clients' experiences of cross-racial therapy. *Journal of Counseling Psychology, 56*, 521–536. http://dx.doi.org/10.1037/a0016905

Chang, D. F., & Yoon, P. (2011). Ethnic minority clients' perceptions of the significance of race in cross-racial therapy relationships. *Psychotherapy Research, 21*, 567–582. http://dx.doi.org/10.1080/10503307.2011.592549

Charmaz, K. (2014). *Constructing grounded theory* (2nd ed.). Thousand Oaks, CA: Sage.

Churchill, S. D. (2018). Explorations in teaching the phenomenological method: Challenging psychology students to "grasp at meaning" in human science research. *Qualitative Psychology, 5*, 207–227. http://dx.doi.org/10.1037/qup0000116

Churchill, S. D., & Wertz, F. J. (2015). An introduction to phenomenological research in psychology: Historical, conceptual, and methodological contributions. In K. J. Schneider, J. F. Pierson, & J. F. T. Bugental (Eds.), *The handbook of humanistic psychology: Leading edges in theory, research, and practice* (pp. 275–296). Thousand Oaks, CA: Sage.

Cooper, H. (2018). *Reporting quantitative research in psychology: How to meet APA Style Journal Article Reporting Standards* (2nd ed.). Washington, DC: American Psychological Association.

Creswell, J. W. (2013a). *Qualitative inquiry and research design: Choosing among five approaches*. Thousand Oaks, CA: Sage.

Creswell, J. W. (2013b). *Research design: Qualitative, quantitative, and mixed methods approaches*. Thousand Oaks, CA: Sage.

Creswell, J. W., Klassen, A. C., Clark, V. L. P., & Smith, K. C. (2011). *Best practices for mixed methods research in the health sciences*. Bethesda, MD: Office of Behavioral and Social Sciences Research, National Institutes of Health. Retrieved from https://obssr.od.nih.gov/training/online-training-resources/mixed-methods-research/

Ditrano, C. J., & Silverstein, L. B. (2006). Listening to parents' voices: Participatory action research in the schools. *Professional Psychology: Research and Practice, 37*, 359–366. http://dx.doi.org/10.1037/0735-7028.37.4.359

Dixon-Woods, M., Cavers, D., Agarwal, S., Annandale, E., Arthur, A., Harvey, J., . . . Sutton, A. J. (2006). Conducting a critical interpretive synthesis of the literature on access to healthcare by vulnerable groups. *BMC Medical Research Methodology, 6*, 35. http://dx.doi.org/10.1186/1471-2288-6-35

Eagly, A. H., & Riger, S. (2014). Feminism and psychology: Critiques of methods and epistemology. *American Psychologist, 69*, 685–702. http://dx.doi.org/10.1037/a0037372

Elliott, R., Fischer, C. T., & Rennie, D. L. (1999). Evolving guidelines for publication of qualitative research studies in psychology and related fields. *British Journal of Clinical Psychology, 38*, 215–229. http://dx.doi.org/10.1348/014466599162782

Farrelly, S., & Lester, H. (2014). Therapeutic relationships between mental health service users with psychotic disorders and their clinicians: A critical interpretive synthesis. *Health & Social Care in the Community, 22*, 449–460. http://dx.doi.org/10.1111/hsc.12090

Fassinger, R. E. (2005). Paradigms, praxis, problems, and promise: Grounded theory in counseling psychology research. *Journal of Counseling Psychology, 52*, 156–166. http://dx.doi.org/10.1037/0022-0167.52.2.156

Fetters, M. D., & Freshwater, D. (2015). Publishing a methodological mixed methods research article. *Journal of Mixed Methods Research, 9*, 203–213. http://dx.doi.org/10.1177/1558689815594687

Fine, M. (2013). Echoes of Bedford: A 20-year social psychology memoir on participatory action research hatched behind bars. *American Psychologist, 68*, 687–698. http://dx.doi.org/10.1037/a0034359

Finfgeld-Connett, D. (2014). Use of content analysis to conduct knowledge-building and theory-generating qualitative systematic reviews. *Qualitative Research, 14*, 341–352. http://dx.doi.org/10.1177/1468794113481790

Fishman, D. B., & Westerman, M. A. (2011). A key role for case studies: Theory building. *Pragmatic Case Studies in Psychotherapy, 7*, 434–439. http://dx.doi.org/10.14713/pcsp.v7i4.1111

Freud, S. (1900). *The interpretation of dreams*. New York, NY: Norton.

Frost, D. M. (2011). Stigma and intimacy in same-sex relationships: A narrative approach. *Journal of Family Psychology, 25*, 1–10. http://dx.doi.org/10.1037/a0022374

Gallagher Tuleya, L. (2007). *Thesaurus of psychological index terms*. Washington, DC: American Psychological Association.

Gelo, O. C. G., Pritz, A., & Rieken, B. (Eds.). (2015). *Psychotherapy research: Foundations, process and outcome*. Vienna, Austria: Springer.

Gergen, K. J. (1973). Social psychology as history. *Journal of Personality and Social Psychology, 26*, 309–320. http://dx.doi.org/10.1037/h0034436

Gergen, K. J. (2014). Pursuing excellence in qualitative inquiry. *Qualitative Psychology, 1*, 49–60. http://dx.doi.org/10.1037/qup0000002

Gergen, K. J., Josselson, R., & Freeman, M. (2015). The promises of qualitative inquiry. *American Psychologist, 70*, 1–9. http://dx.doi.org/10.1037/a0038597

Gergen, M. M., & Gergen, K. J. (2012). *Playing with purpose: Adventures in performative social science*. Walnut Creek, CA: Left Coast Press.

Gilligan, C. (1977). In a different voice: Women's conceptions of self and of morality. *Harvard Educational Review, 47*, 481–517.

Gilligan, C. (2015). The Listening Guide method of psychological inquiry. *Qualitative Psychology, 2*, 69–77. http://dx.doi.org/10.1037/qup0000023

Giorgi, A. (2009). *The descriptive phenomenological method in psychology: A modified Husserlian approach*. Pittsburgh, PA: Duquesne University Press.

Glaser, B. G., & Strauss, A. L. (1967). *The discovery of grounded theory: Strategies for qualitative research*. Chicago, IL: Aldine.

Gomersall, T., & Madill, A. (2015). Chronotope disruption as a sensitizing concept for understanding chronic illness narratives. *Health Psychology, 34*, 407–416. http://dx.doi.org/10.1037/hea0000151

Gough, B., & Madill, A. (2012). Subjectivity in psychological science: From problem to prospect. *Psychological Methods, 17*, 374–384. http://dx.doi.org/10.1037/a0029313

Greene, J. C. (2007). *Mixed methods in social inquiry*. San Francisco, CA: Wiley.

Griffith, A. N. (2016). Trajectories of trust within the youth program context. *Qualitative Psychology, 3*, 98–119. http://dx.doi.org/10.1037/qup0000049

Guba, E. G., & Lincoln, Y. S. (2005). Paradigmatic controversies, contradictions, and emerging confluences. In N. K. Denzin & Y. S. Lincoln (Eds.), *The Sage handbook of qualitative research* (pp. 191–215). Thousand Oaks, CA: Sage.

Hardison, H. G., & Neimeyer, R. A. (2012). Assessment of personal constructs: Features and functions of constructivist techniques. In P. Caputi, L. L. Viney, B. M. Walker, & N. Crittenden (Eds.), *Personal construct methodology* (pp. 3–51). Hoboken, NJ: John Wiley & Sons.

Harré, R. (1991). Metaphysics and methodology. In R. Jessor (Ed.), *Perspectives on behavioral science: The Colorado lectures* (pp. 19–33). Boulder, CO: Westview Press.

Haverkamp, B. E. (2005). Ethical perspectives on qualitative research in applied psychology. *Journal of Counseling Psychology, 52*, 146–155. http://dx.doi.org/10.1037/0022-0167.52.2.146

Hesse-Biber, S., & Griffin, A. F. (2015). Feminist approaches to multimethod and mixed methods research: Theory and praxis. In S. Hesse-Biber & R. B. Johnson (Eds.), *The Oxford handbook of multimethod and mixed methods research inquiry* (pp. 72–90). New York, NY: Oxford University Press. http://dx.doi.org/10.1093/oxfordhb/9780199933624.001.0001

Hesse-Biber, S. N. (2010). *Mixed methods research: Merging theory with practice*. New York, NY: Guilford Press.

Hill, C. E. (2012). *Consensual qualitative research: A practical resource for investigating social science phenomena*. Washington, DC: American Psychological Association.

Hoshmand, L. T. (2005). Narratology, cultural psychology, and counseling research. *Journal of Counseling Psychology, 52*, 178–186. http://dx.doi.org/10.1037/0022-0167.52.2.178

Husserl, E. (1977). *Phenomenological psychology: Lectures, summer semester, 1925* (J. Scanlon, Trans.). Boston, MA: Martinus Nijhoff. (Original work published 1925) http://dx.doi.org/10.1007/978-94-010-1083-2

Josselson, R. (2007). The ethical attitude in narrative research: Principles and practicalities. In D. J. Clandinin (Eds.), *Handbook of narrative inquiry: Mapping a methodology* (pp. 537–566). Thousand Oaks, CA: Sage. http://dx.doi.org/10.4135/9781452226552.n21

Josselson, R. (2013). *Interviewing for qualitative inquiry: A relational approach*. New York, NY: Guilford Press.

Josselson, R., Lieblich, A., & McAdams, D. P. (Eds.). (2007). *The meaning of others: Narrative studies of relationships*. Washington, DC: American Psychological Association. http://dx.doi.org/10.1037/11580-000

Kelly, G. A. (1955). *The psychology of personal constructs.* Oxford, England: Norton.

Kidd, S. A., & Kral, M. J. (2005). Practicing participatory action research. *Journal of Counseling Psychology, 52,* 187–195. http://dx.doi.org/10.1037/0022-0167.52.2.187

Labov, W. (2006). Narrative pre-construction. *Narrative Inquiry, 16,* 37–45. http://dx.doi.org/10.1075/ni.16.1.07lab

Levitt, H. M. (1999). The development of wisdom: An analysis of Tibetan Buddhist experience. *Journal of Humanistic Psychology, 39,* 86–104. http://dx.doi.org/10.1177/0022167899392006

Levitt, H. M. (2015). Interpretation-driven guidelines for designing and evaluating grounded theory research: A constructivist–social justice approach. In O. C. G. Gelo, A. Pritz, & B. Rieken (Eds.), *Psychotherapy research: Foundations, process and outcome* (pp. 445–484). Vienna, Austria: Springer.

Levitt, H. M. (2016). Qualitative approaches. In J. C. Norcross, G. R. VandenBos, D. K. Freedheim, & B. O. Olatunji (Eds.), *APA handbook of clinical psychology* (Vol. 2, pp. 335–348). Washington, DC: American Psychological Association.

Levitt, H. M., Bamberg, M., Creswell, J. W., Frost, D. M., Josselson, R., & Suárez-Orozco, C. (2018). Journal article reporting standards for qualitative primary, qualitative meta-analytic, and mixed methods research in psychology: The APA Publications and Communications Board task force report. *American Psychologist, 73,* 26–46. http://dx.doi.org/10.1037/amp0000151

Levitt, H. M., Bamberg, M., Creswell, J. W., Frost, D. M., Josselson, R., Suárez-Orozco, C., & APA Publications & Communications Board Qualitative Article Reporting Standards Working Group. (2016, August). *Qualitative reporting standards for research in psychology.* Poster session presented at the annual meeting of the American Psychological Association, Denver, CO.

Levitt, H. M., Butler, M., & Hill, T. (2006). What clients find helpful in psychotherapy: Developing principles for facilitating moment-to-moment change. *Journal of Counseling Psychology, 53,* 314–324. http://dx.doi.org/10.1037/0022-0167.53.3.314

Levitt, H. M., Gerrish, E., & Hiestand, K. (2003). The misunderstood gender: A model of modern femme identity. *Sex Roles, 48,* 99–113. http://dx.doi.org/10.1023/A:1022453304384

Levitt, H. M., Kannan, D., & Ippolito, M. R. (2013). Teaching qualitative methods using a research team approach: Publishing grounded theory projects with your class. *Qualitative Research in Psychology, 10,* 119–139. http://dx.doi.org/10.1080/14780887.2011.586101

Levitt, H. M., Motulsky, S. L., Wertz, F. J., Morrow, S. L., & Ponterotto, J. G. (2017). Recommendations for designing and reviewing qualitative research in psychology: Promoting methodological integrity. *Qualitative Psychology, 4,* 2–22. http://dx.doi.org/10.1037/qup0000082

Levitt, H. M., Pomerville, A., & Surace, F. I. (2016). A qualitative meta-analysis examining clients' experiences of psychotherapy: A new agenda. *Psychological Bulletin, 142,* 801–830. http://dx.doi.org/10.1037/bul0000057

Levitt, H. M., Pomerville, A., Surace, F. I., & Grabowski, L. M. (2017). Metamethod study of qualitative psychotherapy research on clients' experiences: Review and recommendations. *Journal of Counseling Psychology, 64,* 626–644. http://dx.doi.org/10.1037/cou0000222

Levitt, H. M., Surace, F. I., Wu, M. B., Chapin, B., Hargrove, J. G., Herbitter, C., . . . Hochman, A. L. (2018). *The meaning of scientific objectivity and subjectivity: From the perspective of methodologists.* Manuscript submitted for publication.

Levitt, H. M., & Ware, K. (2006). "Anything with two heads is a monster": Religious leaders' perspectives on marital equality and domestic violence. *Violence Against Women, 12,* 1169–1190. http://dx.doi.org/10.1177/1077801206293546

Levitt, H. M., & Williams, D. C. (2010). Facilitating client change: Principles based upon the experience of eminent psychotherapists. *Psychotherapy Research, 20,* 337–352. http://dx.doi.org/10.1080/10503300903476708

Lincoln, Y. S., & Guba, E. G. (1985). *Naturalistic inquiry.* Newbury Park, CA: Sage.

Madill, A. (2015a). Conversation analysis and psychotherapy process research. In O. C. G. Gelo, A. Pritz, & B. Rieken (Eds.), *Psychotherapy research: Foundations, process and outcome* (pp. 501–515). Vienna, Austria: Springer.

Madill, A. (2015b). Let a thousand flowers bloom. *The Psychologist, 28,* 656–658.

Madill, A., & Gough, B. (2008). Qualitative research and its place in psychological science. *Psychological Methods, 13,* 254–271. http://dx.doi.org/10.1037/a0013220

Madill, A., Widdicombe, S., & Barkham, M. (2001). The potential of conversation analysis for psychotherapy research. *The Counseling Psychologist, 29,* 413–434. http://dx.doi.org/10.1177/0011000001293006

Maslow, A. H. (1968). *Toward a psychology of being.* New York, NY: Van Nostrand Reinhold.

Maxwell, J. A. (1992). Understanding and validity in qualitative research. *Harvard Educational Review, 62,* 279–300. http://dx.doi.org/10.17763/haer.62.3.8323320856251826

Maxwell, J. A. (2010). Using numbers in qualitative research. *Qualitative Inquiry, 16,* 475–482. http://dx.doi.org/10.1177/1077800410364740

McCrudden, M. T., Stenseth, T., Bråten, I., & Strømsø, H. I. (2016). The effects of topic familiarity, author expertise, and content relevance on Norwegian students' document selection: A mixed methods study. *Journal of Educational Psychology, 108,* 147–162. http://dx.doi.org/10.1037/edu0000057

McLeod, J. (2011). *Qualitative research in counseling and psychotherapy.* Thousand Oaks, CA: Sage.

McMullen, L. M. (2002). Learning the languages of research: Transcending illiteracy and indifference. *Canadian Psychology/Psychologie canadienne, 43,* 195–204. http://dx.doi.org/10.1037/h0086916

Meixner, C., & O'Donoghue, C. R. (2013). Accessing crisis intervention services after brain injury: A mixed methods study. *Rehabilitation Psychology, 58,* 377–385. http://dx.doi.org/10.1037/a0033892

Merriam, S. B. (2014). *Qualitative research: A guide to design and implementation* (3rd ed.). San Francisco, CA: Wiley.

Mertens, D. M. (2010). Mixed methods and the politics of human research: The transformative–emancipatory perspective. In A. Tashakkori & C. Teddlie

(Eds.), *Handbook of mixed methods in social and behavioral research* (2nd ed., pp. 135–164). Thousand Oaks, CA: Sage.

Minges, K. E., Owen, N., Salmon, J., Chao, A., Dunstan, D. W., & Whittemore, R. (2015). Reducing youth screen time: Qualitative metasynthesis of findings on barriers and facilitators. *Health Psychology, 34,* 381–397. http://dx.doi.org/10.1037/hea0000172

Morgan, D. L. (2007). Paradigms lost and pragmatism regained: Methodological implications of combining qualitative and quantitative methods. *Journal of Mixed Methods Research, 1,* 48–76. http://dx.doi.org/10.1177/2345678906292462

Morrow, S. L. (2005). Quality and trustworthiness in qualitative research in counseling psychology. *Journal of Counseling Psychology, 52,* 250–260. http://dx.doi.org/10.1037/0022-0167.52.2.250

Noblit, G., & Hare, R. (1988). *Meta-ethnography: Synthesizing qualitative studies.* Newbury Park, CA: Sage. http://dx.doi.org/10.4135/9781412985000

O'Brien, B. C., Harris, I. B., Beckman, T. J., Reed, D. A., & Cook, D. A. (2014). Standards for reporting qualitative research: A synthesis of recommendations. *Academic Medicine, 89,* 1245–1251. http://dx.doi.org/10.1097/ACM.0000000000000388

Onwuegbuzie, A. J. (2012). Introduction: Putting the MIXED back into quantitative and qualitative research in educational research and beyond: Moving toward the radical middle. *International Journal of Multiple Research Approaches, 6,* 192–219. http://dx.doi.org/10.5172/mra.2012.6.3.192

Osbeck, L. M. (2014). Scientific reasoning as sense making: Implications for qualitative inquiry. *Qualitative Psychology, 1,* 34–46. http://dx.doi.org/10.1037/qup0000004

Parker, I. (2004). Criteria for qualitative research in psychology. *Qualitative Research in Psychology, 1,* 95–106. http://dx.doi.org/10.1191/1478088704qp010oa

Parker, I. (2015). *Psychology after discourse analysis: Concepts, methods, critique.* New York, NY: Routledge.

Pascual-Leone, A., & Greenberg, L. S. (2007). Emotional processing in experiential therapy: Why "the only way out is through." *Journal of Consulting and Clinical Psychology, 75,* 875–887. http://dx.doi.org/10.1037/0022-006X.75.6.875

Paterson, B. L., Thorne, S., Canam, C., & Jillings, C. (2001). *Meta-study of qualitative health research: A practice guide to meta-analysis and meta-synthesis.* Thousand Oaks, CA: Sage. http://dx.doi.org/10.4135/9781412985017

Patton, M. J. (2015). *Qualitative research and evaluation methods: Integrating theory and practice* (4th ed.). Thousand Oaks, CA: Sage.

Pea, R. D. (1993). Learning scientific concepts through material and social activities: Conversational analysis meets conceptual change. *Educational Psychologist, 28,* 265–277. http://dx.doi.org/10.1207/s15326985ep2803_6

Phillips, B. N., Kaseroff, A. A., Fleming, A. R., & Huck, G. E. (2014). Work-related social skills: Definitions and interventions in public vocational rehabilitation. *Rehabilitation Psychology, 59,* 386–398. http://dx.doi.org/10.1037/rep0000011

Polkinghorne, D. E. (1988). *Narrative knowing and the human sciences.* Albany: State University of New York Press.

Ponterotto, J. G. (2005a). Integrating qualitative research requirements into professional psychology training programs in North America: Rationale and curriculum model. *Qualitative Research in Psychology, 2,* 97–116. http://dx.doi.org/10.1191/1478088705qp035oa

Ponterotto, J. G. (2005b). Qualitative research in counseling psychology: A primer on research paradigms and philosophy of science. *Journal of Counseling Psychology, 52,* 126–136. http://dx.doi.org/10.1037/0022-0167.52.2.126

Ponterotto, J. G. (2005c). Qualitative research training in counseling psychology: A survey of directors of training. *Teaching of Psychology, 32,* 60–62.

Ponterotto, J. G. (2006). Brief note on the origins, evolution, and meaning of the qualitative research concept "thick description." *Qualitative Report, 11,* 538–549.

Potter, J., Edwards, D., & Wetherell, M. (1993). A model of discourse in action. *American Behavioral Scientist, 36,* 383–401. http://dx.doi.org/10.1177/0002764293036003008

Potter, J., & Wetherell, M. (1987). *Discourse and social psychology.* London, England: Sage.

Prilleltensky, I. (1989). Psychology and the status quo. *American Psychologist, 44,* 795–802. http://dx.doi.org/10.1037/0003-066X.44.5.795

Rennie, D. L. (1995). On the rhetorics of social science: Let's not conflate natural science and human science. *The Humanistic Psychologist, 23,* 321–332. http://dx.doi.org/10.1080/08873267.1995.9986833

Rennie, D. L. (2012). Qualitative research as methodical hermeneutics. *Psychological Methods, 17,* 385–398. http://dx.doi.org/10.1037/a0029250

Richardson, L. (1994). Writing: A method of inquiry. In N. K. Denzin & Y. S. Lincoln (Eds.), *Handbook of qualitative research* (pp. 516–529). Thousand Oaks, CA: Sage.

Ricoeur, P. (1984). *Time and narrative* (Vol. 1, K. McLaughlin & D. Pellauer, Trans.). Chicago, IL: University of Chicago Press.

Rihacek, T., & Danelova, E. (2016). The journey of an integrationist: A grounded theory analysis. *Psychotherapy, 53,* 78–89. http://dx.doi.org/10.1037/pst0000040

Riley, S. C. E., Sims-Schouten, W., & Willig, C. (2007). The case for critical realist discourse analysis as a viable method in discursive work. *Theory & Psychology, 17,* 137–145. http://dx.doi.org/10.1177/0959354307073156

Rubin, J. D., Bell, S., & McClelland, S. I. (2017). Graduate education in qualitative methods in U.S. psychology: Current trends and recommendations for the future. *Qualitative Research in Psychology, 15,* 29–50. http://dx.doi.org/10.1080/14780887.2017.1392668

Sandelowski, M., & Barroso, J. (2007). *Handbook for synthesizing qualitative research.* New York, NY: Springer.

Shadish, W. R. (1995). Philosophy of science and the quantitative–qualitative debates: Thirteen common errors. *Evaluation and Program Planning, 18,* 63–75. http://dx.doi.org/10.1016/0149-7189(94)00050-8

Shelton, K., & Delgado-Romero, E. A. (2011). Sexual orientation microaggressions: The experience of lesbian, gay, bisexual, and queer clients in psychotherapy. *Journal of Counseling Psychology, 58,* 210–221. http://dx.doi.org/10.1037/a0022251

Small, M. L. (2011). How to conduct a mixed methods study: Recent trends in a rapidly growing literature. *Annual Review of Sociology, 37,* 57–86. http://dx.doi.org/10.1146/annurev.soc.012809.102657

Smith, J. A. (2004). Reflecting on the development of interpretive phenomenological analysis and its contribution to qualitative research in psychology. *Qualitative Research in Psychology, 1,* 39–54.

Smith, J. A., Flowers, P., & Larkin, M. (2009). *Interpretive phenomenological analysis: Theory, method and research.* London, England: Sage.

Smith, J. A., Spiers, J., Simpson, P., & Nicholls, A. R. (2017). The psychological challenges of living with an ileostomy: An interpretative phenomenological analysis. *Health Psychology, 36,* 143–151. http://dx.doi.org/10.1037/hea0000427

Staller, K. M. (2013). Epistemological boot camp: The politics of science and what every qualitative researcher needs to know to survive in the academy. *Qualitative Social Work: Research and Practice, 12,* 395–413. http://dx.doi.org/10.1177/1473325012450483

Steinberg, S. R., & Cannella, G. S. (2012). *Critical qualitative research reader.* New York, NY: Peter Lang.

Stiles, W. B. (1993). Quality control in qualitative research. *Clinical Psychology Review, 13,* 593–618. http://dx.doi.org/10.1016/0272-7358(93)90048-Q

Suárez-Orozco, C., Gaytán, F. X., Bang, H. J., Pakes, J., O'Connor, E., & Rhodes, J. (2010). Academic trajectories of newcomer immigrant youth. *Developmental Psychology, 46,* 602–618. http://dx.doi.org/10.1037/a0018201

Sue, D. W., & Sue, D. (2013). *Counseling the culturally diverse: Theory and practice* (6th ed.). Hoboken, NJ: John Wiley & Sons.

Suzuki, L. A., Ahluwalia, M. K., Mattis, J. S., & Quizon, C. A. (2005). Ethnography in counseling psychology research: Possibilities for application. *Journal of Counseling Psychology, 52,* 206–214. http://dx.doi.org/10.1037/0022-0167.52.2.206

Tashakkori, A., & Teddlie, C. (2010). *Sage handbook of mixed methods research in social and behavioral research* (2nd ed.). Thousand Oaks, CA: Sage.

Tong, A., Sainsbury, P., & Craig, J. (2007). Consolidated Criteria for Reporting Qualitative Research (COREQ): A 32-item checklist for interviews and focus groups. *International Journal of Qualitative Health Care, 19,* 349–357. http://dx.doi.org/10.1093/intqhc/mzm042

Walsh, R. G. (2015). Making discursive space in psychology for qualitative report-writing. *Qualitative Psychology, 2,* 29–49. http://dx.doi.org/10.1037/qup0000020

Wanat, M., Boulton, M., & Watson, E. (2016). Patients' experience with cancer recurrence: A meta-ethnography. *Psycho-Oncology, 25,* 242–252. http://dx.doi.org/10.1002/pon.3908

Wendt, D. C., & Gone, J. P. (2012). Decolonizing psychological inquiry in American Indian communities: The promise of qualitative methods. In D. K. Nagata, L. Kohn-Wood, & L. A. Suzuki (Eds.), *Qualitative strategies for ethnocultural research* (pp. 161–178). Washington, DC: American Psychological Association. http://dx.doi.org/10.1037/13742-009

Wertz, F. J. (2005). Phenomenological research methods for counseling psychology. *Journal of Counseling Psychology, 52,* 167–177. http://dx.doi.org/10.1037/0022-0167.52.2.167

Wertz, F. J. (2014). Qualitative inquiry in the history of psychology. *Qualitative Psychology, 1,* 4–16. http://dx.doi.org/10.1037/qup0000007

Wertz, F. J. (2015). Phenomenology: Methods, historical development, and applications in psychology. In J. Martin, J. Sugarman, & K. L. Slaney (Eds.), *The Wiley handbook of theoretical and philosophical psychology: Methods, approaches, and new directions for social sciences* (pp. 85–101). Chichester, West Sussex, England: John Wiley & Sons. http://dx.doi.org/10.1002/9781118748213.ch6

Wertz, F. J., Charmaz, K., McMullen, L., Josselson, R., Anderson, R., & McSpadden, E. (2011). *Five ways of doing qualitative analysis: Phenomenological psychology, grounded theory, discourse analysis, narrative research, and intuitive inquiry.* New York, NY: Guilford Press.

Williams, E. N., & Morrow, S. L. (2009). Achieving trustworthiness in qualitative research: A pan-paradigmatic perspective. *Psychotherapy Research, 19*, 576–582. http://dx.doi.org/10.1080/10503300802702113

Wolcott, H. F. (2008). *Ethnography: A way of seeing* (2nd ed.). Lanham, MD: AltaMira Press.

Yin, R. K. (2014). *Case study research design and methods* (5th ed.). Thousand Oaks, CA: Sage.

Zimmer, L. (2006). Qualitative meta-synthesis: A question of dialoguing with texts. *Journal of Advanced Nursing, 53*, 311–318. http://dx.doi.org/10.1111/j.1365-2648.2006.03721.x

Index

About the Author

Heidi M. Levitt, PhD, is a professor of clinical psychology in the Department of Psychology at the University of Massachusetts Boston. She was chair of the American Psychological Association (APA) Publications and Communications Board Working Group on Journal Article Reporting Standards for Qualitative Research (JARS–Qual Working Group; Levitt et al., 2018). From 2017 to 2018, she was president of the Society for Qualitative Inquiry in Psychology (SQIP; APA Division 5, Quantitative and Qualitative Methods). In addition, she chaired the SQIP task force to develop a white paper on recommendations for designing and reviewing qualitative research. She has been associate editor for the journals *Qualitative Psychology* and *Psychotherapy Research*. She is an APA Fellow in Division 5 (Quantitative and Qualitative Methods), Division 29 (Society for the Advancement of Psychotherapy), Division 32 (Society for Humanistic Psychology), and Division 44 (Society for the Psychology of Sexual Orientation and Gender Diversity).

APA Style®

www.apastyle.org

Complete Your Collection of APA Style Books

Publication Manual
of the American Psychological Association

The sixth edition offers new and expanded instruction on publication ethics, statistics, bias-free language guidelines, electronic reference formats, and the construction of tables and figures.

284 pages | Softcover | List Price $29.95 | Member $22.46
Visit **www.apastyle.org** for additional formats and pricing.

Concise Rules of APA Style
Sixth Edition

This easy-to-use pocket guide provides complete guidance on the rules of style that are critical for clear communication.

List Price $29.95 | Member $22.46

Mastering APA Style:
Instructor's Resource Guide, Sixth Edition

This guide is designed to help improve students' understanding and use of APA Style before they begin writing research papers and reports.

List Price $29.95 | Member $22.46

Presenting Your Findings
Sixth Edition

Adelheid A. M. Nicol and Penny M. Pexman

This book provides invaluable guidance on the proper table format for a wide range of statistical analyses in an engaging and accessible format.

List Price $19.95 | Member $14.96

Mastering APA Style:
Student's Workbook and Training Guide, Sixth Edition

This is a self-pacing, self-teaching workbook that can be used to learn APA Style quickly and effectively.

List Price $25.95 | Member $19.46

Displaying Your Findings
Sixth Edition

Adelheid A. M. Nicol and Penny M. Pexman

This book offers readers essential guidance on creating figures that effectively present their findings.

List Price $19.95 | Member $14.96

Reporting Quantitative Research in Psychology
Second Edition

Harris Cooper

This new edition presents guidance for applying Journal Article Reporting Standards and Meta-Analysis Reporting Standards for quantitative research.

List Price $29.95 | Member $22.46

AMERICAN PSYCHOLOGICAL ASSOCIATION